THE MUSICIAN'S JOURNEY

The Musician's Journey

CRAFTING YOUR CAREER VISION AND PLAN

Jill Timmons

OXFORD
UNIVERSITY PRESS

OXFORD
UNIVERSITY PRESS

Oxford University Press is a department of the University of Oxford.
It furthers the University's objective of excellence in research, scholarship,
and education by publishing worldwide.

Oxford   New York
Auckland   Cape Town   Dar es Salaam   Hong Kong   Karachi
Kuala Lumpur   Madrid   Melbourne   Mexico City   Nairobi
New Delhi   Shanghai   Taipei   Toronto

With offices in
Argentina   Austria   Brazil   Chile   Czech Republic   France   Greece
Guatemala   Hungary   Italy   Japan   Poland   Portugal   Singapore
South Korea   Switzerland   Thailand   Turkey   Ukraine   Vietnam

Oxford is a registered trademark of Oxford University Press
in the UK and certain other countries.

Published in the United States of America by
Oxford University Press
198 Madison Avenue, New York, NY 10016

Library of Congress Cataloging-in-Publication Data
Timmons, Jill.
The musician's journey : crafting your career vision and plan / Jill Timmons.
p. cm.
Includes bibliographical references and index.
ISBN 978-0-19-986132-3 (hardback : alk. paper)—ISBN 978-0-19-986134-7 (pbk. : alk. paper)
1. Music—Vocational guidance.   2. Music trade—Vocational guidance.   I. Title.
ML3795.T54 2013
780.23—dc23
2012033088

ISBN 978-0-19-986132-3
ISBN 978-0-19-986134-7

9 8 7 6 5 4 3 2 1
Printed in the United States of America
on acid-free paper

to my beloved parents
George and Margaret Timmons: musicians and entrepreneurs

Contents

About the Companion Website

www.oup.com/us/themusiciansjourney

To accompany *The Musician's Journey* we have created a website where readers can access additional information, such as worksheets, questionnaires, and extended discussions.

Foreword

PUBLICATIONS ABOUT LEARNING to play an instrument are many, but useful books about building a profession in the world of performing are comparatively few. Even with the vast range of human expression available through playing music, and despite the many ways to earn a living utilizing one's instrument, it's a stubborn and depressing fact that many talented musicians soar over the hurdles of learning to play poetically, only to stumble when it comes to assembling a rewarding career.

I use the word "profession" in the first sentence advisedly, because it carries a connotation of vocation and suggests lengthy, intensive training. Specialists in the world of performance and teaching have to have both a strong calling to express themselves through the art of their instrument and the willingness to study intensely, at every stage of their career. "Study," too, is a weighty word, because it means not only the work that all musicians undertake practicing the great masterworks and receiving the guidance of top artist-teachers, but also the ongoing search for knowledge through personal investigation, reflection, and cultivation.

The Musician's Journey: Crafting Your Career Vision and Plan sets forth a unique blueprint for success in all these parts of one's profession. Jill Timmons draws inspiration from a wide range of sources—psychologists, novelists, scientists and philosophers ranging from Euclid to Oliver Sacks—all in the service of musicians wanting to find personal fulfillment and financial reward. She describes our musical world as it is, not as we wish it were, and gives us the tools to develop our own unique vision of happy excellence and bring it to fruition.

She, correctly I think, focuses early on the importance of developing an entrepreneurial mindset. This runs counter to the training of many of us, which fosters a mentality of rule-following and a Garboesque "I want to be alone with my art" aloofness. No, says Timmons, engage with the world, develop your own vision and road map, and work it.

I am impressed with the wealth of practical strategies Timmons offers us. The companion website is especially useful, containing worksheets, checklists, and questionnaires. Yet throughout the book runs a thread of reflection and contemplation, and an emphasis on the enriching qualities of the search itself—as long as it is grounded in the realities of our daily lives.

Are you a college student, unsure of your direction? Or a midcareer professional struggling to maintain your artistic vision in a world that often seems to prefer watching the lowest forms of human behavior rather than becoming immersed in great art? *The Musician's Journey: Crafting Your Career Vision and Path* will be a wise and useful friend to you as you build your own path to personal and professional fulfillment.

—Scott McBride Smith

Preface

A NUMBER OF years ago I began a search for the ideal resource for postgraduate musicians looking to put their careers on the fast track. I was looking for an all-encompassing book for my clients, those professionals who were typically mid-career musicians seeking artistic renewal and career development. Many of these clients found themselves at a crossroads professionally, often a moment that required a paradigm shift and a call to reenvision what it means to work as a musician. Although there are countless books that explore the spiritual side of making music, as well as an equally large number of "how to" manuals that offer guidance for all the practical considerations of career management and success, I found nothing that actually joined these two worlds in a way that was both inspiring and practical. In short, I was looking for a book that could guide musicians in the process of creating their career vision and that would also provide concrete strategies for making that career a reality. This book is the result of that search for a comprehensive career guide, one that could be an essential tool for musicians looking to thrive in the most beautiful of professions.

The Musician's Journey: Crafting Your Career Vision and Plan addresses the process of developing an artistic vision, designing a plan for that vision, becoming an entrepreneur within the global market place, and understanding how we change and adapt through the innate resources of the human brain. The genesis for this book came from my personal experiences as a practicing concert pianist and educator for the past thirty years. Over the course of that time, I expanded my work to include mentoring other musicians. These clients are primarily professional musicians who are seeking change, renewal, support, validation, or simply a witness to their growth and development. Essentially, these are artists who want a more authentic connection to their personal career goals and dreams along with a practical plan of action, one that will allow them to thrive in the music industry. Most of these clients are midcareer professionals and often their work involves changing career direction, sculpting new career activities, or realizing long-held dreams. It has been my honor and privilege to work with these inspiring musicians and to share their wisdom with others.

Along with examples from the work of clients, colleagues, and myself, I have also included in this book much of what other authors have to say about the music profession and the larger context, the life of an artist. I have drawn on the wisdom of poets and pundits, scholars and scientists, visionaries, philosophers, and especially those authors who give credence to living with vitality and creativity. My hope is that from these abundant sources, any musician can find support and guidance in creating that thriving career in music.

Perhaps the information presented in the following chapters will also offer what Ralph Waldo Emerson so valued: "A chief event of life is the day in which we have encountered a mind that startled us." You may want to use *The Musician's Journey* as a source for a new career paradigm; a paradigm that is not fixed in time but functions eternally. Each chapter begins with an inspiring literary quote, to set the stage so to speak. Although the book project began in 2000 (an abundant economy, riding the dot-com wave, good times), I have found the research to be timeless, apart from any specific economy. At this point, we are having the worst recession since the Great Depression. We know, however, that musicians are needed at all times, that young people can have expanded brain function through making music, that music therapy is now effectively aiding those who suffer from dementia, that we can stave off the effects of aging with musical activities, and that we can turn to the beauty of music to nurture our souls.

A thriving musical career can often be fueled in effective ways from a number of sources, including the guidance of experienced mentors, what is effective for others in the field, and insights from seemingly disparate disciplines. Finding that outside information can often shorten the timeline for launching a dynamic career. For that reason, I have included many divergent sources from my research and have chosen those authors that present a provocative and stimulating discourse that may serve to inspire you with new ways of envisioning and creating a dynamic career path.

As I developed *The Musician's Journey*, I chose a conversational voice, much as I would use in relating to a client. I imagine you, the reader, joining me in conversation about ways that we can create new career paths and possibilities. Although there is considerable research presented in the book, I have purposefully avoided the more formal tone of academic prose. You will find humor as well as pathos. My narrative it is not comprehensive to be sure, but rather strives to ignite the transformative process within a musician.

Whether we are responding to the vagaries of our external world or that richly textured inner artistic life, we are referenced from our personal intentions, those tightly held passionate hopes and inspirations that we have in mind. Career development truly begins with how we envision ourselves amidst the world around us. To be consciously aware of what drives us as artists is critical to finding a rewarding career path.

The people who will best benefit from this book are those musicians who have completed the bulk of their formal training. As we develop our skills and talents during our apprentice years, there are many time-consuming and pressing issues to consider, such as building proficiency on an instrument, acquiring a broad foundation in music, and exploring those first professional opportunities. Toward the end of our professional training we are then ready to consider more fully those emerging career issues. We need proficiency as artists before we are capable of envisioning who and what we can be.

Ideally, the reader is one who has been in the music business for a while, and thus is able to draw upon a body of rich professional experiences. This type of musician is often seeking to thrive in imaginative and diverse ways, independent of such mega artist managers as Columbia Artists, ICM (International Creative Management), and the like. This book is not for the handful of "superstars" in the music industry but instead offers those musicians who don't fit this mold a way of living their career dreams. In Chapter 9, "True-Life Stories," you will find examples of widely diverse careers: from jazz to classical artists, composers, and interdisciplinary professionals, all with their own unique career journey.

The Musician's Journey presents topics directly related to individuals and their collaborative colleagues. I have chosen to avoid the topic of the collective and group matters such as the sociological functions of reference groups or how systems theory might be applied to musical organizations and populations. I am, however, interested in the view of anthropologist Margaret Mead: "Never doubt that a small group of thoughtful committed people could change the world. Indeed, it's the only thing that ever has."

In this book you will find suggestions for how to address the process of envisioning your career as well as strategies for creating a concrete plan of action. From exploring the science behind the adaptability of the brain to the nuts and bolts of a successful business strategy, I offer many resources that may also inspire you to continue your research and inquiry far beyond the narrative in this book. I hope *The Musician's Journey* will ignite a transformation in your thinking about what it means to be a musician and how to thrive in that career, ultimately sharing your knowledge and acumen with others.

In beginning our conversation about a music career, we can draw upon much wisdom available outside our industry. In his inspiring book *Journey of the Heart: The Path of Conscious Love*, John Welwood imagines life in a twofold structure. He also speaks to how we live as artists.

> In larger cosmic terms, human life unfolds on the edge where heaven and earth meet. Our very posture—feet firmly planted on the ground and head raised toward the open sky—perfectly depicts our twofold nature. At the same time our upright head and shoulders enable us to see far-off things—horizons, stars, suns, planets and the infinite reaches of space all around. Half of our life is about taking our seat on this earth and creating structures (such as home, family, work) that further our unfolding. No matter how grand our hopes, dreams, or visions, putting them into practice always involves grappling with the limitations of our culture, our body and personal history, and our emotional temperament. The other half of life involves surrendering to what is beyond us, letting go of the structures we have created, and continually moving forward into new, unknown areas. The heaven principle working in us calls on us to expand, develop larger vision, and explore greater possibilities, beyond what we already know or see right in front of us. It indicates the way in which the human spirit is vast and open like the sky, never entirely encompassed by personality, the limitations of conditioning, or the constraints of form and matter.[1]

Welwood's vision can direct us to think in new ways regarding what it means to have a career in music. Our artistic vision and plan will be both spiritual and concrete, truly joining heaven and earth.

Whether you find yourself at the beginning of an envisioning process, whether you are unearthing long-held dreams, or discovering that your vision is in place and that now you need guidance in crafting an effective plan, you will find an abundance of resources in this book. From vision to plan is a vast continuum requiring different strategies at various junctures. Most of all, this process requires imagination and desire. As artists we eventually come to discover that this vision–plan continuum is repeated many times throughout our lifetime. Through this continuing spiral of renewing our artistic vision and plan, we have the opportunity to delve deeper into our work as artists, finding a richly textured life of service and beauty. I hope this book will inspire you to create an artistic vision and craft a plan to realize your own thriving career in music. This is the musician's journey.

Acknowledgments

NO BOOK COMES to fruition without the wisdom of outside readers, skilled editors, and the wise counsel of friends and colleagues. *The Musician's Journey: Crafting Your Career Vision and Plan* benefited from many generous individuals. While not all can be noted here, some can be recognized for their significant contribution. My gratitude extends to Ellen Summerfield, Sarah Wider, and Rhonda Ringering for their careful reading of the earliest drafts; to Linfield College for giving me that all-important sabbatical to write the book; to Terry Mandel for her marketing wisdom; to Marian Biscay for insights into brain function; to Faun Tiedge for her generous collegiality and support; to John O'Malley for his grant-writing acumen; to Nancy Lynch for her somatic education; to Steve Peterson for his Internet savvy; to Mark Wickman for his wise business advice; to Lauren Pelon and Laura Klugherz for their inspiring stories; to Janie Webster for editing those final revisions; and to all the clients and colleagues who gave so generously in their "true-life stories." My gratitude extends also to the thousands of flourishing music entrepreneurs I have encountered throughout the years. You have been my greatest inspiration.

Oxford University Press made this book possible. I wish to extend a special thanks to my acquisitions editor, Todd Waldman, whose wisdom, talent, and humor inspired me at every revision. The staff at Oxford are, without a doubt, the gold standard in our business.

Lastly, I owe a debt of gratitude to my husband, Sylvain Frémaux. This book would not have been written without his loving support.

THE MUSICIAN'S JOURNEY

Artists love to immerse themselves in chaos in
order to put it into form, just as God created form
out of chaos in Genesis. Forever unsatisfied with
the mundane, the apathetic, the conventional,
they always push on to newer worlds.

—ROLLO MAY[1]

1

A CAREER IN MUSIC

MUSICIANS AND THEIR WORLD

The call to be a musician is both awe-inspiring and daunting. Anyone in this industry knows that the highs and lows can be extreme. One day you are on top of the world with great reviews, a successful audition, a place at the helm in the nonprofit world, or a fine performance to your credit. The next day can bring funding cuts, staggering competition, professional politics, job loss, disappointment, and heartache. And yet those of us who choose this life know that there is no better path. Through being a musician, we are called to our own destiny and that of the collective. Through the language of music, musicians offer society a framework for empathy, imagination, and the creation of something that will exist beyond one's own lifetime. Music can also serve to mirror and explain culture. We can come to know different times, traditions, and places through music. Music can be predictive, since art springs from the unconscious levels, anticipating future social and technological developments, like science fiction writers or in the case of music, like the composers of the fifties and sixties who forecasted the future mainstream use of electronic technology.

As individual artists, musicians are challenged to know who they are, their place in the world, their special "calling," and to somehow realize their vision in practical terms. Ultimately it is a life of service. We are called to the sacred and archetypal journey of the hero. Joseph Campbell, in *Transformations of Myth Through Time*, identifies the hero's journey as a metaphor for our own psychological life, the internal life of the soul.

The concept of myth as archetypal story is universal. Whether in the Arthurian legend, the Japanese ideal of the samurai, or the Jewish stories of Esther or King David, heroes are distinguished by daring and bravery. This tradition of fearlessness is central to being an artist and is essentially grounded not only in being courageous

I

about external challenges, but also most importantly in being fearless about who you are. Authenticity, courage, bravery, imagination, energy, compassion, patience, receptivity, empathy, humor, and fortitude are the minimum requirements. In archetypal terms, this is the powerful integration of the masculine and feminine principles. With this awareness, if we are to set out on the hero's journey, we must be prepared to slay our illusions, understand ourselves honestly, and grasp how the brain functions in support of this journey. Chögyam Trungpa, in his guide to living a sacred and heroic path, *Shambhala: The Sacred Path of the Warrior*, directs the artist to become a warrior. Here the term warrior does not refer to aggression or violence but, rather, "one who is brave."

> The key to warriorship and the first principle of Shambhala vision is not being afraid of who you are. Ultimately, that is the definition of bravery: not being afraid of yourself. Shambhala vision teaches that, in the face of the world's great problems, we can be heroic and kind at the same time. Shambhala vision is the opposite of selfishness. When we are afraid of ourselves and afraid of the seeming threat the world presents, then we become extremely selfish. We want to build our own little nests, our own cocoons, so that we can live by ourselves in a secure way.[2]

So the life of a musician is no ordinary path. We have responsibilities to our own destiny, our own soul-making, and we must simultaneously reach out to our own time and place to bring to humankind the numinous experience that music can provide. Discussions regarding career matters can seem mundane indeed and for some, overwhelming. And yet, as John Welwood describes in the preface of this book, we are the connection between heavenly and earthly matters. If we are to prosper as musicians, we must integrate our inspired personal artistic vision with the practical matters of career building. Most musicians are challenged with bringing these two aspects into harmony and balance. Ideally, a musician can follow a personal visionary path and at the same time attend to such earthly concerns as career development, income production, project development, consortium building, and the like. With clear artistic vision and a well-designed action plan, musicians can thrive in the music industry, realizing that intersection between "heaven and earth" that Welwood describes.

THE WORLD OF MUSIC: WHERE WE ARE TODAY

Volumes have been written on the value and efficacy of music. Music has been referred to as the "universal language." Scholars and musicians alike know that music has been central to humankind dating back to prehistoric sources. Jacques Chailley, in *40,000 Years of Music: Man in Search of Music*, suggests that evidence in the famous prehistoric wall paintings at Ariège, France, leads us to believe that music was part of these early cultures.[3] Throughout the ages, humans have used music to celebrate, worship, ignite feelings, and respond through movement. Music touches the soul in ways that are universal, arcane, and at the same time fully present in this moment. As a temporal art form, music draws us into being completely engaged in the moment either through the performance of music or in the role of audience member.

Music goes hand in hand with myth and may actually be a kind of glue that permeates culture and joins individuals to the collective. As Peter Kalkavage observes in his provocative essay "The Neglected Music: Why Music Is an Essential Liberal Art," "Music does not merely sound. It casts a spell and conjures worlds. Music is no mere addendum to human life, no historical accident that might just as well have never been, but an essential part of who we are as human beings."[4]

There is an abundance of writing available on the subject of music. Music permeates contemporary societies on a world scale from commercial applications to important uses in cultural rituals. Writings on musical topics include, for example: the intrinsic value of music to society and the education of the young; the power of experiential learning and the creative and imaginative experiences that come from making music; and descriptions of new applications for diseases such as those described as dementia. At the same time, the music industry in the United States continues to struggle for support, musicians bemoan the lack of job opportunities, and our culture has a long history of underfunding public school music programs.

It is well known even to those outside our profession that over the course of the past three decades we have seen a gradual decline in public support for the arts. Federal and state dollars for the arts have diminished considerably, and in spite of the well-documented data available on cognitive and interpersonal benefits of a music education, the public school sector rarely holds daily music classes or a full complement of ensembles: choir, band, and orchestra. The reasons for this are complex. The overriding circumstances, however, have to do with how schools are funded in the United States. Roughly half of public school funding comes from local government budgets. How the local tax base fares in terms of revenue can often determine what financial resources are available for music electives. In addition, there is now a much greater emphasis in public school education on accountability through testing, particularly in the areas of reading, writing, and math. On the other hand, most private K–12 schools, commanding substantial tuition fees, regularly include an array of visual and performing arts options to attract the discerning parent. If you doubt this disparity between the public and private sector, I urge you to examine the music budgets and programs in your own locale.

One of the standards of democracy has always been equal education for all, both in quality and access. As Americans, we are still far from this model. By comparison, most small communities in Western European countries (France and Germany, for example) have well-established funding programs for the arts. The philosophy that drives this type of national support for the arts stems from an intrinsic commitment to the general populace and from the belief that all citizens have the right and necessity for equal access to the arts. In France, for instance, the bulk of funding goes not to some fiscal entity in Paris. Rather, there is an intricate system, beginning with the Ministry of Culture, that filters funds to the *région*, the *département* (or county), and finally to the city. Even if you are living in one of the remote communities of the Auvergne, the rich and inspiring world of the arts is available. Bill Ivey, former chairman of the National Endowment for the Arts, identifies our national challenge regarding arts support as one of renewal:

> If our shared purpose is to build a public good by shaping an equitable, open, and exciting arts system, we must first paint a picture of that ideal landscape, then create public policy and private practice that will make our dream a reality. Nearly a half-century ago, arts leaders crafted just such a vision of a cultural landscape enriched by a deeper connection among the fine arts, citizens, and communities, and they found a way to realize that dream. We must take up the challenge again and shape a new model for supporting the arts in the next half-century.[5]

If musicians, educators, and scholars are to create new avenues of support and value for the arts, expand our vistas as creators and innovators, educate our young people to greater possibilities in experiential learning, and enrich our communities in humanizing and inspiring ways, then we must take up the challenge of reinventing ourselves, our careers, and our profession. Our world has altered and the rate of change continues to accelerate. Technology has brought us to the doorstep of distant cultures and musical traditions. The boundaries between art music, vernacular sources, and global voices have blurred; there are no longer clear demarcations. As artists, we are called to imagine new possibilities for creating music, teaching music, and performing music. To thrive in this new millennium, musicians will need to develop innovative paths to reach their goals. The terrain is different and finding our way requires a new road map, one that is built from pioneering strategies and novel resources. In fact, musicians may find that they actually build the road as they go.

Our new cultural landscape of the twenty-first century is complex, pluralistic, global, and culturally diverse, and changes at a dizzying rate. We did not get here overnight, however, and the music industry has taken a hit along the way. With arts funding in crisis, with a complex and global market place, and with the instant rewards and distractions of technology, musicians are challenged to respond in new and innovative ways as they bring the inspiration of music to disparate communities. I believe that the changes that must be made to bring music and the arts to the forefront of access and funding will ultimately begin with artists themselves. It's that old adage from the sixties: think globally; act locally.

We can no longer assume that our communities and institutions will fully fund those music programs and the artists that are vital to the health and well-being of a civilized society. To meet the challenge of funding and innovation, a new paradigm is required, one that includes: arts advocacy, community outreach, development of our own income base, preparation of our students for the world of technology, and the development of consortia with other artist–educators. As musicians, then, we have several mandates to fulfill: certainly to follow our own destiny as artists but also to bring the value and beauty of the arts to various populations. In addition, we must reeducate the American public as to the power and necessity of the performing arts. As musicians we are both artists and educators. We are privileged to share our knowledge and provide service: service to the composer, service to our students, and service to the broader community through the enrichment and beauty of music. For many, we are the gateway to the numinous experience.

Robert Johnson, a noted Jungian scholar, defines the experience that the arts can provide as "ecstasy." It is the experience that gives joy to life. In his book *Ecstasy: Understanding the Psychology of Joy*, he suggests that, "Unlike the ephemeral state of happiness, joy is a lasting value that nourishes and sustains the spirit as well as the body. Joy does not induce a craving for more, because it is enough. The glow of ecstasy enlivens every living thing. And, in the fiery glow of ecstasy, joy can be born within us."[6] This is what music can offer.

As artists, we are in the forefront of fighting for the soul and civility of our culture. We are pioneers and trailblazers lighting the way. Johnson understands that art can serve as a powerful ritual. Through works of art we can glimpse the spirit. "Through the arts, as with ritual and ceremony, we can live out those parts of ourselves that can have no practical expression. In this sense both art and ritual are, paradoxically, ways of doing something but not doing it. We satisfy the inner urge without doing external damage.... The arts have always been a source of ritual for humankind, a way to express the inexpressible."[7] In creating our own prosperous careers as music professionals, we serve humankind, thereby offering society something of inspiration and transcendence.

A THRIVING CAREER IN MUSIC: THE NEW NORMAL

In the area of career development, the notion of reinventing ourselves and responding to new markets is not new. Today, you can find numerous books, blogs, journals, websites, and even tweets that offer excellent resources. The bibliography of this book is but a mere appetizer. Generally, however, career resources in music fall into two categories. The first represents those materials that deal with the spiritual side of music, the creative process, igniting the Muse, finding your voice as a musician and developing your personal artistic vision. James Jordan's exquisite book *The Musician's Soul: A Journey Examining Spirituality for Performers, Teachers, Composers, Conductors, and Music Educators* is one of the best examples about this area. The second category is characterized by the "how to" approach. It might be euphemistically entitled *Music Careers for Dummies*. Publications and resources abound that offer concrete guidance in such topics as how to make a business model or business plan, how to enlarge your teaching studio, book more concerts, write a bestselling teaching series, develop your grant-writing skills, create media materials for your work, and so on. All of the above resources and more are essential in creating that new path towards a richly rewarding career.

What I believe is missing in the current body of resources for musicians, however, is a guide that addresses one's artistic vision and outlines a methodology of how to create a concrete plan that will realize that vision. I call this the vision–plan continuum. This chronological process is something that artists continually revisit over the course of a lifetime. We first craft our artistic vision and then put into action our strategic plan. Along this continuum we may find that our challenges vary. Sometimes we are stymied as to how we clarify our artistic vision. At other times, we may be in a conundrum as to how we can put forth our vision with all manner of business considerations. Occasionally, however, our vision–plan continuum brings us to moments in our lives where we are able to harvest the fruits of our labor, knowing that we have reached our goals and that we are living out our dreams. These moments of achievement can serve as a kind of artistic plateau and often provide rich experiential information about the next step in our career. A harvesting period can also give us powerful validation for the path that we have chosen, all the while knowing that we will once again in the future return to that vision–plan continuum.

The American existential psychologist Rollo May offers a descriptive metaphor for this process. In his book *Love and Will*, May uses the terms "intention" and "will" to flesh out what is essential for the creative act. "Intention" is that notion of what we wish to create—that unique personal artistic vision. "Will" is that force within that brings to fruition those dreams of what could be. It is the self-actualizing principle that finds concrete expression in our actions. We cannot thrive as musicians unless we join these two worlds.

Meeting the challenges of the twenty-first century clearly requires a paradigm shift. No longer can we assume that there will be that all-encompassing job waiting for us if only we go to the right school, study with the right teacher, and practice, practice, practice. How do you get to Carnegie Hall? In your own car! By the same token, we can no longer plan on inheriting the careers of our predecessors.

Preparing today's musicians means training them to make their own careers. Through my own work as an artist–educator, from the wisdom of many talented clients, gifted colleagues, and with advice and counsel from numerous mentors and wise teachers, I know it is possible to have a rich and rewarding career in the music industry. Whether you are a burgeoning concert artist, an innovative teacher, writer, arts administrator, or closet entrepreneur, there is a wealth of opportunity awaiting you if you know how to craft your own personal vision and develop a concrete plan that serves that vision.

These are exciting times with greater possibilities. We must, however, reinvent ourselves, seek new support for our work and our businesses, expand our outreach, and develop new strategies to thrive in the music industry. I offer this work as a way of helping others to connect with their inner vision and to implement a dynamic plan of action, thereby building their own unique career path. This process of self-discovery works. As Carl Jung said, "I don't believe, I know." I know it is possible.

All the time. It is miraculous. I even have a superstition that has
grown on me as a result of invisible hands coming all the time—namely,
that if you do follow your bliss you put yourself on a kind of track
that has been there all the while, waiting for you, and the life that you
ought to be living is the one you are living. When you can see that, you
begin to meet people who are in your field of bliss, and they open doors to
you. I say, follow your bliss and don't be afraid, and doors will open where
you didn't know they were going to be.

—*The Power of Myth: An Interview with Bill Moyers*, JOSEPH CAMPBELL

2

NEWS FROM THE FRONT

MOST ARTISTS ARE familiar with Joseph Campbell, his inspiring interviews with television journalist Bill Moyers, and his subsequent book, *The Power of Myth*. Campbell has much to teach us about the artist's path and how it best unfolds. He directs us to "follow our bliss," aligning ourselves with our true artistic path, living in authenticity, and avoiding those personal fears that can plague us. By trusting in our inner wisdom, by being consciously aware of what gives us joy and passion, Campbell knows that in creating our "field of bliss," serendipity can play a strong role in how our career unfolds. Doors open, opportunities come forward, and we discover a kind of resonance in our efforts. We know that we are creating a career that is a clear reflection of who we are, with all our skills and talents in abundance. And yet, as most artists know, living this kind of courageous life is rare.

Having worked with a vast array of clients over the course of the past thirty years, I have discovered a theme that often surfaces for those musicians who are searching for a more authentic and vibrant career. Many of those midcareer professionals express despair at the loss of their original joy and sense of purpose in music. In a very real sense, their despondency is at the soul level, reflecting a deep and personal anguish over the absence of that earlier experience of joy. My teacher, György Sebök, liked to say that by the age of ten, children are visited by gremlins at night. While they are sleeping snuggly in their beds, those "bad fairies" declare: "Playing the piano is very difficult!" His amusing metaphor illustrates so well how cultural conditioning, standardized education, and the traditions of the past can squeeze the joy and space out of the creative process—that manifestation which is infinite, divine, and abundantly present in young children.

So what happens to artists from the time they are children until they leave those professional training institutions? Frequently, our children are stifled by overly critical parents, rigid private teachers, contests with *winners* and *losers,* the overburdened public school classrooms, and an education system that has endless skills and competencies as the arts are systematically being dismantled. Too often, teachers are corralled into teaching to the test and with a particular emphasis on math and reading competencies. Still, there are countless hardworking and dedicated teachers who do their very best once the classroom door is shut. They are highly skilled in giving minimal attention to the paperwork and assessments required by the state. Instead, they connect with children in creative and inspiring ways.

When young musicians head off to college or university, the stakes become incrementally higher. Winning often becomes the measuring stick, and we find many students entering a fiercely hierarchical environment. Professors have "power" over students: their grades, scholarships, opportunities, and information. It is the rare college or university whose ethos focuses on what Martin Buber calls the "I and Thou" relationship. It is what Buber describes as placing ourselves completely in relationship to another, without pretense or any conceived notion of outcome. There is no control involved and in fact such a relationship is neither static nor constant. A true dialogue unfolds and the bond that is created serves to enlarge each person.

James Jordan, in *The Musician's Soul*, eloquently describes the limitations of many current educational philosophies. He believes that a college education often stresses the importance of enabling the student to exploit the power aspect of reality. "To some degree, they [colleges and universities] try to develop his/her ability to appreciate beauty. But there is no education for the sublime. We teach children how to measure, how to weigh. We fail to teach them how to revere, how to sense wonder and awe." Jordan goes on to quote Abraham Joshua Heschel from *God in Search of Man.* "The Greeks learned in order to comprehend. The Hebrews learned in order to revere. The modern man learns in order to use it."[1] Without care and awareness, higher education can be a place of soul loss, abuse of power, and a distortion of what is fundamentally important for the study of music: acquiring proficiency as a musician; developing an awareness of beauty and the numinous; and experiencing the power of music-making both individually and collectively.

Traditionally in the United States, there has been little or no training as to why one makes music, how one connects to the numinous experience, or how one creates a career based on a personal artistic vision and purpose. By the time I see clients, many are firmly established in outer-referenced values. "How was that performance? Did *you* like what I just played? Will this be sufficient for my new CD? Will this win me the audition/job/contract/competition/scholarship? How *do* I win?" (an external judge can decide?). After many years, however, this way of life can wear thin. The artist within us longs to be free and autonomous. Is it any wonder that many talented people eventually get fed up with the current system of outer-referenced values and choose to leave the music profession altogether?

Of course if we are lucky, we find a few great teachers who somehow are able to exist in both the university/conservatory system as well as the spiritual world of music making. They are in it but not of it. These extraordinary educators are most often practicing artists themselves. They have not lost touch with the creative act, nor have they let their souls wither among the reports, curricular revisions, assessments, auditions, and juries on which many academics focus. These teachers are able to carry on as artists while tending adequately to the practicalities of administration and accreditation. These savvy souls know that young people come to study music because they are passionate about making music, and that their educational experiences are best when this is supported. Visionary educators also understand that there should be no hierarchy in higher education because the educational process is a copilgrimage between professor and student. It is the essence of the "I and Thou" relationship that Buber so beautifully describes.

These gifted teachers are like powerful beacons to young artists. They are quite rare in higher education because they sit on the razor's edge between being an artist and an academic. They live in the hierarchical world of education with its curricula, accreditation, assessment, governance, and politics, while at the same time providing all the commitment, independence, passion, and absorption that an artistic life requires.

There are, however, possibilities within higher education if one can artfully traverse the rocky shoals. Colleges, universities, and conservatories can be terrific environments to learn a craft, providing you have a visionary artist/teacher. One can acquire new information, test oneself before entering the "real world," and develop lifelong professional friendships and contacts. During a four-year degree program, most students have that singular moment in their lives when they can devote full attention to themselves. And there are those rare programs that offer a unified and inspiring curriculum.

On a national level, we need to look more closely at the powerful efficacy that arts training provides to our students of all ages. Our global economy is challenging us as a nation to provide greater creativity and innovation within our workforce. As a nation, we can no longer rely solely upon the production of goods and services, depending upon cheap labor, raw materials, or reliable financial systems and the flow of money. We must now turn to dynamic innovation as a way to compete effectively in the world market place. For this, we must turn to arts education. In a recent article in the *San Diego Business Journal* author John Eger writes eloquently about the need for integrated arts education. He quotes several specialists in the field. Former US Secretary of Education Richard Riley offers this insight. "The jobs in greatest demand in the future don't yet exist. In fact, they will require workers to use technologies that have not yet been invented to solve problems that we don't yet even know are problems. Clearly we are headed into a new and uncertain future, yet many of the critical questions are not being asked, let alone answered, in the public debate over K–12 education."

Adding to this debate, Dana Gioia, chairman of the National Endowment for the Arts, said, "If the U.S. is to compete effectively with the rest of the world in the new global market place, we need a system that grounds all students in pleasure, beauty and wonder. It is the best way to create citizens who are awakened not only to their humanity, but also to the human enterprise that they inherit and will—for good or ill—perpetuate."[2]

We also know from current brain research about the positive effects that music education can provide, enhancing math and science comprehension, not to mention experiential learning by collaboration and creativity within groups. As our students engage in professional training at the college or university level, they will need adequate preparation for future job markets, especially the ones that have yet to exist. For those artists, however, who have already completed their professional training and are looking to recreate themselves, or who are responding to a sense of soul loss, there are other factors in play.

Working with clients over the course of many years, I discovered that most of the initial inquiries I received were for some sort of instrumental coaching. Sometimes it was for an upcoming performance, audition, or recording. Often when artists are seeking the change that can bring a renewed sense of purpose and vigor to their professional work a comfortable place to begin is with the study of their instrument. For those clients seeking a deeper connection with their work and an authentic and dynamic career, however, those coaching sessions often moved into the territory of soul loss. By "soul loss" I refer to that experience of living life without a sense of authenticity. Vitality and that feeling of being alive are missing. For musicians this can be a life that is primarily outer referenced. In other words, it is doing things for the wrong reasons; perhaps in response to the demands of others, or preconceived notions of what constitutes a winning career in music and more importantly, an irrational response to long held, if misguided, caveats that define success.

Most of my individual clients have been adult musicians who have completed their advanced training, having been in the profession for ten to twenty years as both performers and teachers in varying proportions. These heroic clients have been engaged in every corner of the music profession and some have even held "day jobs" outside the industry. They invariably showed up at the first meeting expressing grief concerning their artistic lives, often with dissatisfaction that has been long-standing. They frequently describe earlier attempts to remedy a growing sense of distress. Sometimes they try to resolve an unsatisfactory career path by changing jobs, reengaging in applied study, moving to a new locale, developing new marketing strategies, and so on. Nevertheless, something is often missing for these artists and, in essence, many find that they have reached a kind of insurmountable wall. They intuitively know they must do something, or wither. Almost without exception, our first meeting involves expressions of grief, a sense of the "last straw," the recounting of painful stories about artistic or educational traumas they had suffered, or simply ongoing disappointment. These courageous individuals arrived at my doorstep asking for serious help, guidance, and mentorship. This has been my greatest experience as an artist/teacher, to meet so many heroic, passionate, dedicated artists interested in their own transformation. It has been my greatest learning and indeed the copilgrimage of a lifetime. Working with these contemporary clients has required a willingness on my part to share myself without reservation, applaud their courage and vulnerability, learn all that I could about the creative process, and endeavor to be a skilled listener, not just to the words people offered but what their bodies said. Lastly, I had to be willing to authentically share my own journey as an artist.

Over the years, I have developed many ideas and theories about working in the music industry, concepts and strategies that are key factors in developing a thriving career. In working with clients I eventually distilled my response to their question "Can you help me?" by producing a questionnaire for all new clients. This hastened our connection, it informed me about each person long before we met, and it gave the client an idea about the nature of the mentoring process. The following is that questionnaire which you can download from the companion website and print out for your own use.

 EXAMPLE 2.1

CLIENT QUESTIONNAIRE

1. What are your professional goals for the next five years? Do you have a five-year plan or are you in the process of crafting your vision?
2. What are three heartfelt goals that are central to your work and who you are as an artist/teacher?
3. What do you see as the most obvious barrier to your success?
4. What do you find missing in your current strategy to achieve your goals? (for instance, additional education, networking, funding, professional contacts, visibility, and so on)
5. What would you consider your best successes? In what do you excel? What has been your "finest hour"?
6. What is your most urgent and pressing professional need at this time?
7. How do you see me helping you?

The questionnaire also provided a starting point for career development. These questions are designed to gather information that may be outside the conscious mind. They also serve to disrupt rigidly held beliefs. Because outside sources can enlighten artists to new frontiers and provide crucial innovative information, I also commonly provide new clients with a reading list designed to address their particular questions and challenges. Depending upon where a client finds themselves on the vision–plan continuum, I look for sources that will not only provide inspiration and concrete strategies but, more importantly, ideas that can nudge and tease them into a paradigm shift. I often begin with Jordan's *The Musician's Soul*. In this tightly written narrative, Jordan is supremely eloquent in calling musicians to create a path that is uniquely their own.

Jordan suggests first starting with stillness in order to connect one's imagination, intuition, and intention. He suggests that to know and love yourself as a unique soul is essential in becoming an artist. And like many, Jordan knows that musical study and performance are first and foremost acts of service. As musicians, we endeavor to resonate with the composer. In our work we must provide the utmost depth of preparation, commitment, passion, and fidelity to all that we do. Without this grounding, we cannot make a plan for our professional goals and dreams— certainly not one that will be effective or that will last. To attempt a short cut for this journey will result only in frustration and disappointment. Real success comes from inner referencing, connecting to our authentic process, and a state of awareness.

Outer referencing, conversely, can often send us in the wrong direction, buffeting us from idea to idea, and luring us into the backwaters of what others may deem successful. Inner referencing provides a very different sort of map. It's very much like traveling in a foreign country. If you don't have a good map (your plan of action) and your destination clearly marked (your vision), you can end up getting horribly lost. Paris is my favorite city. I never drive there without considerable preparation, detailed directions, and a good cup of coffee. If you are not careful, you can get trapped on the Périphérique (the beltway). Inner referencing, by contrast, sends you in the right direction, excellent map in hand. Even if you have a few detours (there is *always* road construction in Paris!), or you take an occasional wrong turn, you still know where you are headed and you simply check your map. You might also stop for a quick patisserie and another cup of coffee simply to fortify yourself for the journey.

Whether you are moving from soul loss to a thriving career or if you are simply beginning your journey towards professional fulfillment, there are a number of ways to prevail, creating that vibrant and dynamic career. As Joseph Campbell suggests, however, it is a journey defined by being inner referenced (following *your* bliss). This process embraces serendipity; it requires courage and the ability to seek new information, and a trust in your own wisdom. Indeed, my own career has been a virtual road map of accidents, luck, chance encounters, all the while continuing with my preparation and learning.

THE ACCIDENTAL ENTREPRENEUR

I have been fortunate in the music business, having discovered an enriching and thriving career for myself. I have also witnessed the success of many individual artists who have taken charge of their careers. I came to the music business, however, having never won a major competition, living in a primarily rural western state (Oregon), initially having no artist management, no personal fortune, and no single "big break" to launch my career. In short, I began my professional journey quite ordinarily. I was like countless other well-trained musicians looking to make a career in the field I loved best. I was able to develop my career because I realized early on that being a musician and making a living were two different activities. At times they intersected, but not always. As my career unfolded, I discovered that I was in fact living the life of an entrepreneur.

I pursued the traditional track of education in piano performance: Bachelor of Arts and Bachelor of Music, Master of Music, and the Doctor of Musical Arts. I began my journey as a professional musician early in my high-school years, pursuing jobs as an accompanist, as a pianist for musical theater, a church musician, a member of a classical piano trio, and as a musician who would accept just about any gig that would pay. I even had a stint as a lounge pianist during graduate school. My parents were both musicians and with a large extended family of like-minded professionals, I had plenty of encouragement and support.

My goal was to perform; I loved playing the piano, and the more varied experiences I encountered, the more I discovered about my career path. Much to my surprise, as I completed my formal education as a classical pianist, I discovered that concerts became more plentiful, I eventually acquired artist management, and the world of touring opened to me. These were heady years with funding from the National Endowment for the Arts, appearances throughout the world, and tours throughout the United States that included the National Gallery of Art, Carnegie Recital Hall, Merkin Hall, and the Dame Myra Hess series in Chicago. Eventually my work expanded to Europe and South America. I also enjoyed exciting and stimulating partnerships with other music professionals, building lifelong friendships and collaborations.

Early in my career, I also landed an artist-in-residence position at Linfield College in Oregon. This small liberal arts institution has been a key element in my career mandala. When I was hired, Charles Walker was serving as the visionary college president, leading Linfield into the 1980s. Although my position had the title of "artist in residence," I also functioned in a tenure-track position as professor of music. I was fortunate in those early years to work for a college president who loved music and who supported cutting-edge ideas around curriculum development and student engagement. He challenged me to reach for the stars. I was truly lucky to work for and with Charlie Walker for ten years. I was honored that he readily used my skills and resources in support of the college's mission.

From my own career, I discovered that the music profession holds an abundance of extraordinary "jobs" for musicians. That even though I wasn't Horowitz, I could have a very satisfying and reputable performance career, one in which I could be proud. I saw opportunities for intersecting the professional world of performance with that of academia. My career was much larger in scope than my college position but because of that, my contribution to academic life became richer. For example, I have been able to regularly bring international colleagues to campus, organize performance series, engage my students in master classes with campus guest artists, and remind my students that their training years are just the beginning of life as an entrepreneur.

As my career unfolded, I also realized that there were many artists throughout the country successfully making a living, and not just from one gig to the next but often through "streams of income." Even though I had a full-time academic appointment, the early days of my career began to expand from that post and I too developed those streams of income. Early in my career as a touring artist, I often marketed myself to small rural arts councils as the K-Mart of pianists: a good product at a discount price. It always got a laugh and I had fun making connections with presenters in this way. Let's face it, the superstars in our industry are probably not going to focus on educational residencies, intersect with retirement communities, or provide a string of concerts throughout rural America. The need is there, however. Underserved communities often need assistance in developing their community music programs, training school children, arranging musical events, working with technology to connect their community to the rest of the world, and preparing young people for vibrant musical careers. As one of my wise colleagues once said: "When you consider all the music that needs to be played, there just aren't enough musicians!"

Intersecting teaching and performance has always been my passion and the nexus of my career vision. In following that dream, my career has unfolded in surprising and extraordinary ways. I eventually went on to include recording projects of underserved composers, bicultural musical collaborations, international partnerships, teaching residencies, writing, consulting, and I even did a stint as a music journalist. I also discovered that if you follow your passion and apply a strategy for realizing your vision then things will unfold naturally. Serendipity and synchronicity serve to sculpt those career opportunities and choices, leading to a kind of "new musician's road map."

One leading American performing artist who best exemplifies an innovative career path, that new musician's road map, is pianist Gilbert Kalish. He has his finger on the pulse of how careers are made. Kalish is an icon in the field of art music. He is director of performance activities and codirector of the Contemporary Chamber Players at the State University of New York (Stony Brook), a consummate recording artist, a champion of contemporary music, and is a much sought-after collaborative artist. In addition, he has served on the faculties of the Tanglewood Music Center, the Banff Center, and the Steans Institute at Ravinia. At the Ravinia Festival in 1999, classical music broadcaster Bruce Duffie did a radio interview with Kalish, which revealed much about this exceptional pianist's career.[3] To read a transcript of the full interview on Duffie's website, use this link: http://www.bruceduffie.com/kalish.html. The following is an excerpt from that inspiring interview.

GK: I'm very content with what I've done. I'm astonished. I never expected it. I grew up alone in my musical world. It was important for my mother that if you had a child with a gift, that it be developed, but she didn't really know a lot. And I went to public schools. I went to Columbia University. I didn't go to Juilliard. I didn't go to a music school. I studied privately and somehow slipped into the profession. I didn't do competitions. I didn't do any of that! I slipped into the profession sort of on the shoulders of having learned and loved chamber music. Then I was feeling really curious about new music. I married young and felt, "I have to make a living," and this was one outlet because other people were not doing it. The people at Juilliard were not doing it because their teachers were teaching them the old war horses and they were going for competitions. I just was not taking that route. I somehow got in on the periphery and did new music and chamber music. Somehow that led me to my solo work of Ives, and then back to my roots, where I studied what I studied when I was a youngster—the great masters. Then came the opportunity to do Haydn and to do chamber music with the Boston Symphony Chamber Players for thirty years, with my colleagues in the Juilliard Quartet, with Jan DeGaetani. We met as youngsters and we were in a new-music group together, and just did recitals because we were curious young people and we wanted to do recitals, so we did recitals. I remember I had a series at Swarthmore College and I said to Jan, "I can't offer you more than seventy-five dollars, but I can tell you that I'll rehearse as much as you want. Let's do a recital." And you know, out of nothing, all these things somehow developed. You learn. So therefore, always my advice to the people I deal with is just do the best work you know how in whatever you're doing. Somebody will hear you and will say, "Oh, that's good stuff!" There'll be concentric circles in your life; one will lead to another and that's how you'll make your way. I don't think most people make their way by being stars. That's not a happy way, either. If you're a star, you're a star. Okay, that's great if you have that kind of immense gift and you can take the pressure. But otherwise there are lots of gifts in music; there isn't one gift. There are many different kinds of gifts. I always think the most important thing is to enjoy what you're doing. Do it to the best of your ability, no matter the circumstance! I have many little pathways that finally led me to a very satisfying life. I learned the Ives Violin Sonatas with a young violinist named Paul Zukovsky. He was about nineteen and maybe I was twenty-five. I didn't know why I was learning them. He was curious; he pushed me to it and I said, "Sure, you think it's interesting. Let's do it." We went to the library and looked at the manuscripts, and we learned the four of them. So this monumental kind of effort went into doing these pieces, but I was young, and I had time to do it because that's what I was doing. We played in this church in Brooklyn, and who cares? There were maybe sixteen people in the audience. All this work and there's nobody there! At the end of the concert, some-body comes up and he says, "I am Sam Charters. I work for Folkways Records and I am a fanatic follower of Ives. I do folk recordings for Folkways. I go in the mountains of Kentucky and Tennessee and get people who are in Appalachia doing their things. But they let me do anything I want and I want to record you guys in all these sonatas." I thought he was crazy, but he did record us. And somebody else picked that up, and we did it in New York and got a huge spread in the *New York Times*!

BD: Out of a little audience of sixteen people!

GK: Out of that; just because you do the work because you want to do it. What happens, happens. I'm not Pollyanna. I don't think it's like that, but it really is the truth—you can't make it happen. The only thing you can make happen is that you do well, that you do what you do with love and integrity, and then you see what happens.

I like very much Kalish's view of making music, living from the inside out in terms of what motivates and inspires, and especially choosing a path that includes rich and savory collaborations with others. His humility and gratitude serve to under-score his keen awareness of serendipity and how thorough preparation favors those moments. The idea that we are both careful in our preparation and planning and at the same time letting go of the outcome brings into play the paradox of what musi-cians do. When we hold on too tightly to outcomes, we may actually miss the real career opportunities that serendipitously come to us. Desire and joy can provide a rudder to our ship, steering us in the right career direction. Look to those musical experiences that provide you with vitality and inspiration, and as Kalish suggests, do what you do with love and integrity. Be open to the outcome. For many musi-cians, this is truly a paradigm shift.

A CALL TO CHANGE

For the artist who has experienced soul loss, it can be a difficult journey back to that childhood place; the reason that most of us were first drawn to music—beauty and the numinous experience. The angst, anxiety, and pain of soul loss can be the first wake-up call and the first step toward creating one's vision. It is that "depression" that can serve as a possible impetus to change. If we are truly aware of our despair and avoid blaming the outer world, we can move forward. It is essentially our soul's call to return to vitality, purpose, and meaning in our lives.

Many artists, especially as they head towards midlife, have "awakening opportunities." These are occasions that disrupt our sense of routine, inevitability, and safety. They can upset the status quo and often engender a sense of anxiety or even fear. These defining moments can, however, serve as powerful beacons for change. I believe that with time and practice we begin to actually welcome these clarifying moments because we come to understand that new adventure and self-discovery await us. These opportunities are by their very nature challenging but they bring with them enormous psychic energy, enrichment, and serendipity.

By responding to these awakening opportunities, we discover that it is never too late to embrace change, ignite transformation, and embark on a new adventure—one of the soul. You can create a richly rewarding career in music. There are concrete strategies to help you achieve your vision, to manage it, to survive financially, and to claim your rightful place as a unique and gifted artist. This book offers you a way of launching your own dynamic career. By following your bliss with a clear artistic vision and a concrete plan of action, you can move forward. By learning how to operate as an entrepreneur in today's market place, you can bring to fruition your own professional dreams and goals. In doing so, I invite you to reconsider many preconceived notions of what a music career entails and how you can achieve your vision and goals as an artist.

3

MUSICIANS AND THE PATH OF ENTREPRENEURSHIP

Stages
As every flower fades and as all youth
Departs, so life at every stage,
So every virtue, so our grasp of truth,
Blooms in its day and may not last forever.
Since life may summon us at every age
Be ready, heart, for parting, new endeavor,
Be ready bravely and without remorse
To find new light that old ties cannot give.
In all beginnings dwells a magic force
For guarding us and helping us to live.
Serenely let us move to distant places
And let no sentiments of home detain us.
The Cosmic Spirit seeks not to restrain us
But lifts us stage by stage to wider spaces.
If we accept a home of our own making,
Familiar habit makes for indolence.
We must prepare for parting and leave-taking
Or else remain the slaves of permanence.
Even the hour of our death may send
Us speeding on to fresh and newer spaces,
And life may summon us to newer races.
So be it, heart: bid farewell without end.[1]

WHEN I LEFT home for my university studies, my mother gave me this poem by Hermann Hesse (reprinted by permission of Henry Holt and Company, LLC). I found it to be both inspiring and frightening. Be ready for parting, new endeavors, things may not last forever, life after death?! Yikes! As I checked with my friends, I realized that other mothers were not sending their high-school graduates off into the world with such poetic declarations. Looking back over all the years since, I now realize that it was the most important departing gift she was to give me. Not surprisingly, I have kept her manual typewriter version with me ever since. It has become a kind of touchstone. In that symbolic moment of leaving home I clung to my well-thought-out plans for success, the friends I already knew at the university, the classes I would take, the professors I would study with, where I would live, even where I was going to graduate school, following what I knew would be a stunning academic undergraduate education; definitely "a home of my own making." My mother knew otherwise and that life would be sending me into a maelstrom of change and metamorphosis.

This glimpse from Hesse about the nature of existence taught me to balance the contemplative life of an artist with the demands of an active life that seeks self-realization, much in the same way that Welwood describes in the preface of this book. It would be many years into my own career, however, before I fully understood Hesse's profound revelation regarding the duality and conflict than can exist between the visionary life and one of self-realization in the practical world. Ultimately, what I discovered through simply living my life as an artist is that Hesse calls us to integrate these two polarities—to move beyond duality. It is that joining of heaven and earth.

In the amalgamation of these two polarities, we are required to be self-aware, inner directed, practical in the ways of the world, and continually returning to how our imagination is made manifest in the world. When artists avoid duality in their thinking they are then free to think critically, solve problems with imagination and originality, experience passion for something in music, and make a sustained commitment to that passion. Lastly, they are able to welcome ongoing change and uncertainty, relishing those creative and serendipitous opportunities that arise. In short, an artist becomes an entrepreneur and for these musicians a new road map is essential.

PREPARING TODAY'S MUSIC ENTREPRENEURS

I define music entrepreneurship as the ability to create and sustain a viable career in the music industry. A music entrepreneur is one who is able to generate a personal vision for a dynamic career and who has the necessary training and skills to construct and put into action a plan for that vision. Music entrepreneurship is the dynamic outgrowth of our changing culture, a culture that is pluralistic, interdisciplinary, global, and often representative of the small-business model. According to the US Small Business Administration Office of Advocacy, in its September 2009 report, "There are an estimated 29.6 million small businesses in the United States alone. These businesses employ just over half of the country's private sector workforce, they include 52 percent of all home-based businesses, and they represent 97.3 percent of all identified exporters and produced 30.2 percent of the known export value in 2007. Most importantly, these small businesses generate a majority of the innovations that come from United States companies."[2]

It is clear that music professionals are now facing a culture and an economic environment that favor the entrepreneur.

Still, many young musicians successfully complete their professional training but are stymied as to how to proceed with a career. This is due, in part, to the nature of professional training in the United States. How many colleges, universities, or conservatories prepare their music students to think outside the box in terms of building a career, being financially successful, and having the courage to do what they really want? The College Music Society (CMS) has been on the forefront of introducing workshops and conferences on the topic of entrepreneurship and bringing to the professional community an awareness of the need for this curriculum. Within our changing society and the new economy, colleges and universities are now challenged to add an entrepreneurship curriculum to their music degree programs in the face of shrinking budgets and diminished resources. Many institutions, such as the University of California (Los Angeles), New York University, Manhattan School of Music, the New England Conservatory, the Eastman School of Music, the University of Colorado at Boulder, and the University of Southern California, have moved forward with innovative entrepreneurship programs. At the time of this writing the CMS has developed a new national initiative regarding music entrepreneurship and has been a leader in codifying this new area of study. In 2007, writing on behalf of the Brevard Conference on Music Entrepreneurship and CMS, Dr. Gary Beckman, director for Entrepreneurial Studies in the Arts at North Carolina State University, offered an overview and rationale for a rigorous approach to entrepreneurship education.

America's music schools are adopting entrepreneurship education at a steady rate. However, the lack of an accepted definition or conception of entrepreneurship has spawned a diverse range of curricular structuring. Concurrently, a lack of scholarship concerning these efforts has buttressed perceptions of entrepreneurship education in music as business education for music students. With new and progressive literature on entrepreneurship emerging from the economic, cognitive and social sciences, many music entrepreneurship programs (and students) have yet to reap the rewards of this scholarship. As this field emerges, developing a solid intellectual foundation is critical to the success and sustainability of these efforts.[3]

Some of our training institutions are beginning to respond effectively to the growing demands from the public sector for better and more appropriate professional training. From this intellectual foundation, however, must also emerge an experiential component that provides our students with hands-on training and that responds swiftly to our rapidly changing economic culture and the future job markets our students face.

Within music degree programs, faculty often teach to standards and accreditation, relying on guidelines from the National Association of Schools of Music and the College Music Society. There is enormous diversity within the music industry, an ever-evolving market place, and a rate of change that is dizzying. From highly theoretical studies, to jazz and the vernacular, to musical theatre and film-score production, we have an ever-increasing spectrum for music professionals who hold a vast array of diverse professional visions. We can no longer expect our students to follow archaic career models. Their future is firmly grounded in the market place. And for those musicians who have already established their musical careers, higher education has rarely offered support for retooling, reimagining, or reinventing a career at midlife.

The *Chronicle of Higher Education*, in the February 17, 2006 issue, presented a compelling view of that market place. In his bracing article "Leaving the Village," Thomas Benton posits that those working in academia need to make a radical shift in regards to what he terms the "sordid market place." Benton offers the following idea: "It's time for most of us—and I am thinking in particular of younger academics—to abandon the genteel pose of being aloof from the sordid market place. We should stop acting as if we were monks, destined for a lifetime of cloistered self-denial. Once you realize there's a world outside the academic village, almost any future seems possible." Having one foot in that "sordid market place" and one in the ivory tower, I sometimes marvel at the distance that has been inherent between these two realities. This may be why there is such a strong national entrepreneurship initiative from the CMS, bringing our training institutions into closer harmony with the professional world.

Through entrepreneurship, we develop a new musician's road map—fluid, imaginative, highly personal, rigorous, demanding, and amazing. With this new map in hand, we can face a tough economic climate or ride the wave of prosperity—either way we know how to respond quickly and imaginatively. With severe budget cuts, cost-cutting measures, and concerns for stable financial support for the arts, strategies are needed that can lay the groundwork for lifelong learning and development for music entrepreneurs, preparing our students, clients, and colleagues to continually respond to undetermined future markets.

As we educate our students for an entrepreneurial market place, we must do so within the context of musical and intellectual rigor as well. Tradition and excellence meet innovation and imagination. Sometimes it is useful to consider more profound questions for the students we teach, such as: What is your personal vision as a musician? Why are you here? What are your dreams and goals? Do you have a plan to realize that vision? At this juncture, one of my standard questions to my college students is, "What would your perfect life look like ten years from now?" This enlists a host of responses and goes far beyond "What is your major?"

For the emerging entrepreneur who may be still exploring career options or sources for inviting the Muse, turning first to the issue of personal vision can sometimes begin with a provocative reading list—books and publications that get the creative juices flowing. Several excellent sources are: Joe Dominguez and Vicki Robin, *Your Money or Your Life: Transforming Your Relationship with Money and Achieving Financial Independence*; Richard Bolles, *What Color is Your Parachute? 2012: A Practical Manual for Job-Hunters and Career-Changers*; and Thomas Moore, *A Life at Work: The Joy of Discovering What You Were Born to Do*. Each of these groundbreaking publications presents an iconoclastic view of why and how we work, providing an excellent starting point in casting a career vision.

Professional musicians today know that one's formal music education is just the beginning, and often what we learn becomes quickly obsolete, much like computer technology. As Hesse reminds us: "We must prepare for parting and leave-taking / Or else remain the slaves of permanence."

At the heart of all great entrepreneurs is the understanding that first one must have a vision of what one wishes to accomplish. As successful artists, scholars, and teachers we all know the power of a dynamic and creative vision. Most thriving musicians undoubtedly have a success story that emerged from their own artistic dreams: an important audition, a successful grant proposal, job interview, publication, performance; the list goes on. Their vision was put into action through careful planning, hard work, and often serendipity. Entrepreneurs know that opportunity favors the prepared individual. Bottom line, however, we must realize that our careers are in our hands, that we must work creatively to develop opportunities, acquire the necessary skills for those careers, and be flexible, engaging in lifelong learning. We no longer look to our jobs as a career. Rather, each job we have can become part of the rich kaleidoscope of an ever-changing and evolving career.

THE BENEFITS OF ENTREPRENEURSHIP

The world of entrepreneurship requires each of us to expand our belief system about the music profession and what it can be. Today we are called to develop our own musician's road map. The rewards, however, are abundant. Nancy Uscher, in her pioneering book *Your Own Way in Music: A Career and Resource Guide*, offers this inspiring description of what entrepreneurship can offer musicians. "How precious it is to feel vital! To wake up in the morning full of excitement about a project, a job, or an endeavor that poses both challenge and reward. We all have the right as well as an obligation to ourselves to be ambitious, to discover and develop gifts throughout life, and to be single-minded—even downright stubborn—about realizing our most important aspirations, even if it means forging a path as yet undiscovered."[4] Her vision of life as a music entrepreneur may or may not include a single job; it may be the life of a freelancer and it may include different streams of income. No matter, those choices are driven by the inner direction of a creative artist, and a vision and plan that drives their work—a true entrepreneur. Later in the book we will examine the particulars of how we create a vision for ourselves and craft our detailed and effective plan of action.

4

PREPARING FOR CHANGE

SOMETIMES IN LIFE we must make the proverbial "paradigm shift" in order
to discover new truths or create new realities. Exploring change, exercising one's
imagination, engaging in lifelong learning and creative thinking, and encounter-
ing the numinous experience all can lead to discovering who you are as an artist.
Undoubtedly this work is not something that is casually done over a weekend
retreat, or by reading a particularly inspirational book, networking with esteemed
colleagues, or jumping on a trendy bandwagon. The brain holds on to what is known
and familiar. Hermann Hesse knew this so well. Frankly, if change were easy, we
would readily (and happily) engage in this process! Maybe that's why Emerson so
valued a mind with a fresh idea, that "mind that startled us." Emerson was invigo-
rated with new information, not recycled platitudes.

So a book that addresses the quest for our own personal vision and the concrete realization of that vision must first prepare the reader to embrace change.
An effective way to do this is to look at how the brain works when faced with
a personal call to the transformative process. All roads lead back to the brain
and what some scientists refer to as the "mind/brain." Creativity and planning
use the whole brain and require deft traversing of the two brain hemispheres via
the *corpus callosum*, that thick white band of nerves that connects those two
hemispheres. How do we use our brains more effectively, how do we avoid getting trapped in the storms of the limbic system, exactly where is my "higher
thinking" (frontal lobes)? I need new and fresh ideas. Where are they? Einstein
said, "Imagination is more important than knowledge." You might look there.
Detachment, paradox, nonlinear time, and a quantum view of how we affect our
reality will be important considerations in looking at the brain, and in particular,
brain neuroplasticity.

So it seems that the conversation has wandered into the woods of esoteric ideas about the human brain; and what does this have to do with simply finding a job in music, or developing a thriving career? Keep reading.

BRAIN NEUROPLASTICITY: A PERSONAL STORY

Neuroplasticity. There's a word you can sink your teeth into, and since the 1970s it has become a vibrant hotbed of research and discovery. What scientists used to tell us was that the brain is a rather fixed organ. Past childhood, we must live with basically who we are, a fixed entity with a small margin of opportunity for change—certainly no possibility for quantum change. I often used this belief as a convenient excuse as to why I would most likely never be fluent in French. Poor me, I just got started too late…

But experience taught me otherwise, and so I intuitively and experientially came to discover that drastic change, dramatic shifts, and entirely new ways of being were available to me. I first stumbled upon this discovery of brain flexibility out of desperation (that is usually the mother of most change). I wanted to transform my work as a pianist. I was in my early thirties, done with all formal education through the doctoral level. I had performed countless concerts but I knew something was missing. I wanted a deeper connection with the music, a greater understanding of the composer at hand, and an expanded array of resources to realize these goals. I reconnected with my teacher György Sebök. One summer I chose to attend his month-long retreat for pianists in the Swiss Alps. Ernen Musikdorf was the perfect location for a retreat of this sort—some 9000 feet up, in the heart of the Swiss Alps, nestled in the tiny village of Ernen, just a stone's throw from Brig and the Italian border. I dreamed of hours of practice, stimulating conversations with colleagues, sage advice from my teacher, evening walks through Alpine meadows, and a renewed sense of purpose and artistry. Little did I know what was awaiting me.

I arrived in Ernen after some thirty hours of travel: air travel from Portland to New York to Geneva; train from Geneva to Brig; cog rail train to Ernen. Altitude sickness greeted me upon my arrival and for three days I hovered around my chalet. I was assigned practice quarters in the local priest's house and in the bomb shelter of the village. In retrospect this was strangely ironic since what I was to face was a sort of artistic nuclear holocaust and only divine intervention could save me.

I came prepared with several major works from the piano repertoire and I signed up for all the chamber-music opportunities that were available. Sebök had the solo piano coaching in the morning and after lunch. Evenings were for the pleasures of chamber music. The participants were professional musicians from around the world, mostly in the early and middle years of their careers. Sebök also attracted a large following of auditors, those who did not participate in the master classes but who were in rapt attention to every nuance of what Sebök had to say, whether in regard to a performance issue, a technical solution, or a topic from further afield, such as quantum physics. There were many who came simply to be in the presence of this extraordinary artist and teacher.

When it came time for me to receive my first coaching in the public master class, I chose Chopin's F Minor Fantasie. I had played it on numerous occasions but continued to wrestle with the deeper meaning of this austere, passionate, and transcendent work. In short, it had eluded me for quite some time. Following my performance of the Fantasie for the master class, I felt that it had gone about as well as it could have but again, I wasn't really satisfied. The first words out of Mr. Sebök's mouth were: "What are you afraid of?" It was like putting my finger in the wall outlet. Zap! I felt my head spinning and my face becoming very warm. What was he talking about? In a spare, rather detached delivery, Sebök explained that I wanted to control everything and that my fear was in playing wrong notes. It choked off my musicality and my ear. He then said that following the master class he wanted to meet with me privately to speak about this more. Sucking all the oxygen out of the room, I agreed.

Later that day he gave me a series of tests at the piano and concluded that I had an excellent ear but that fear of mistakes was what I needed to overcome. He outlined a regime that I might consider in my practicing and seemed most encouraging by declaring that he felt that I was a person who exhibited a lot of courage and that I could make the necessary changes to free myself. I was on top of the world, I had a plan, things could be fixed in no time, I would be free—*voilà!* there was the change I was seeking.

My elation, however, was short lived following his departing comment: "Of course if one has no fear, one does not need courage." And so began the dismantling of who I was, why I played the piano, how I connected with the music, how I shared that music with others, and, in short, how I lived my life as an artist. What I experienced in that master class was so profoundly jarring ("a mind that startles us") that during the night following the lesson, I had a vivid and powerful dream. That dream has stayed with me.

The dream placed me in an octagonal room with eight doors. All the doors were the same, each painted white with substantial molding. There were no particular identifying features to distinguish one door from the other. I wasn't sure which door to open so I decided to simply open the door in front of me. That door opened into the universe. I awoke to the most incredible feeling of expansion and joy.

The power of Sebök's teaching was in creating a container of trust, providing no particular agenda, simply serving as a vulnerable mirror to my process, and remaining compassionately detached. Incidentally, these are all qualities of a great master teacher. On my side of the equation, I had sufficient desire for change to put fear aside, to be open to whatever he might say, and to say to myself, "what the hell!" Of course once I descended into the proverbial rabbit hole, like Alice, I was never the same. You can't ever really go back once you have had a "mountain" experience. Sebök opened my eyes and pointed me in the right direction. He also taught me about the power of humility. I was required to recognize and live with the powerful emotions and processes that come with those calls for change that are central to the growth of an artist.

And so what does this narrative have to do with brain neuroplasticity or, more precisely, the brain's ability to form new neural connections based on the changing internal and external circumstances of the human being? Everything! Of course at that time I didn't think, "Gee whiz, I will now have to rely on my innate brain adaptability to change myself." Quite the opposite, I felt like one of those early explorers heading to the New World—with nothing but a tiny boat. Sebok's teaching had revealed to me another way of being an artist, living a life that could be more expansive and authentic. It would require deep personal change on my part and although I had a kind of map, or rather a sketch of one provided by Sebök, I would be taking this journey alone. So I began the journey of a thousand miles with the first step—I decided to play, play, play. I got a manager, I divided the work between her and myself, and I performed everywhere. Playing became the lab and I was putting together experiment after experiment. How did I feel before, during, and after a concert? Could I pinpoint those performances that had a glimpse of the numinous? What caused things to go wrong (missed notes, memory slips, a lack of vitality)? The popular Zen saying "The way out is through" most certainly spoke to me. Music is a temporal art form and without entering into the temporality of the concert, we can never know who we are in that moment. There is no rehearsal for the concert! Gradually over several years things began to change, or rather, I began to change. What did I observe? My brain was indeed different. I felt differently about music, I had stumbled upon what it meant to connect with the numinous and I was like an archeologist, digging deeper and deeper for those hidden treasures that the earth does not give up easily.

This process of transformation was not a contained event that I would leisurely revisit as time went on. It became the benchmark of my life and because of the power of this experience, I could no longer move forward in my life in the old ways. I found myself seeking out challenging and transformative opportunities. I worked with several counselors to discover more deeply what the field of psychology had to offer. When one such psychologist told me about brain plasticity I knew I had struck gold. It was what I suspected intuitively. There was a science to confirm my experience.

My prior understanding of brain function was in keeping with the mainstream understanding before the 1970s that the adult brain was not capable of neural regeneration. The old adage "You can't teach an old dog new tricks" was *de rigueur* and until very recently, most scientists believed the brain to be hard-wired instead of flexible and regenerative. Brain research, however, has given us a new normal and we now know those earlier assumption were false.

DEFINITIONS

In this chapter I have purposefully drawn on the wisdom and discoveries of scholars and scientists in the field of brain research. I have loaded the narrative with evidence to support what I know experientially to be true. In doing so, I offer this compelling information as a new genesis for personal change and transformation. Enjoy what these great minds have to offer you.

Since the 1970s, brain neuroplasticity has been a widely accepted area of scientific research, contributing to a vastly new conception of how the brain functions. This plasticity is defined by the brain's capacity to change connections and behaviors within neural networks and by the neurons themselves. This flexibility is in response to sensory stimulation, new information, or injury, and within these neural networks reorganization is possible. The brain indeed can grow new neurons, and create new neural pathways. In their groundbreaking article "The Musician's Brain as a Model of Neuroplasticity," Thomas Münte, Eckart Altenmüller, and Lutz Jäncke describe how neuroplasticity allows the brain to adapt to environmental factors that cannot be anticipated by genetic programming. "The neural and behavioural changes that are attributed to plasticity have been observed on different timescales, ranging from several minutes to the whole lifetime of the individual. Different processes are likely to support plastic changes at the extremes of this timeline. Accordingly, experience-driven neuroplasticity has been explained by both the *de novo* growth and improvement of new dendrites, synapses and neurons."[1] In other words, our brains are capable of regeneration, renewal, and reorganization. We aren't stuck, we can change, and we can imagine new futures and realize those possibilities. Furthermore, according to the research, musicians' brains are also a model of neuroplasticity, and the authors cite MRI evidence for anatomical differences in the brains of musicians compared with control groups—the primary motor area and the cerebellum differ in their structure and size in musicians. So not only is transformation physiologically possible but musicians already have a predisposition for this process.

Exploring cross-cultural research, there are new and exciting dialogues emerging in the scientific community regarding brain neuroplasticity. In 2004, The Mind and Life Institute and his holiness the Dalai Lama presented "Dialogues between Buddhism and the Sciences: Neuroplasticity, the Neuronal Substrates of Learning and Transformation." Richard Davidson, writing the overview presentation for the five-day conference describes the intersection of science and consciousness.

> The brain is not static but rather is dynamically changing and undergoes such changes throughout one's entire life. The scientists assembled for this meeting represent the various levels of analysis in which these questions are being pursued. Research on structural plasticity will reveal how the literal composition of the adult mammalian brain is constantly changing and will show the factors that influence these changes. Other studies at the molecular level reveal how the chemistry of DNA can be changed by experience in ways that affect the expression of our genes. Moreover, such effects on the chemistry of DNA can be produced by social experience, which in turn modifies gene expression in ways that can persist for the duration of a lifetime. These findings have radical implications for conceptualizing the dynamic interplay between nature and nurture.[2]

The Mind and Life Institute conference addressed the role of contemplative training in transforming the emotional mind as well as the nature of mental training and its potential impact on the brain and behavior, with mental training being more prevalent in contemplative cultures than in the Western scientific tradition.

What scientists suggest as essential for this neuroplasticity is that the brain has good oxygen flow and that the brain is constantly challenged by or engaged in diverse, new, and stimulating experiences. The notion of "use it or lose it" is central to brain neuroplasticity. What better way to develop and retain this plasticity than through playing a musical instrument?

Neuroplasticity and change are also reinforced through practice. Think of it this way. When you repeatedly do a certain action, hold a rigid belief structure, or simply revisit a familiar behavioral attitude, the brain develops little ruts or neural pathways. The more practice and repetition the more these pathways are ingrained. Have you ever noticed how difficult is it to change a habit? That habit probably has a significant neural pathway. But because the brain is regenerative, new pathways (i.e., new behaviors, beliefs, experiences, etc.) can be created, and as we engage in this generative process, the old pathways are either modified or they die away, thereby strengthening memory, learning, and most importantly, adaptation. In short, we can, at any age, form new habits and learn new things.

If we subscribe to this new possibility for change and adaptation, then the brain's neuroplasticity can bring us to wholeness. In her riveting and expansive book

The Secret Dowry of Eve: Woman's Role in the Development of Consciousness, Glynda-Lee Hoffmann posits that as humans we are designed to function with a whole psyche. Symbolically this can be expressed by the integration of the masculine and feminine archetypes. Back to the hero's journey—it is one towards wholeness. "The journey to wholeness is not through external means, but by internal means, by recognizing and growing the power of insight, awareness, and recognition in the brain and psyche. Insight is an activity of germ energy within the human psyche, helping us to expand awareness, develop autonomy, and realize wholeness through neural growth and fecundity."[3]

The brain's four neural structures or cortexes (listed in order of evolutionary continuum: reptilian cortex, limbic system, neocortex, and prefrontal cortex) do not always work in harmony, however. This neural predisposition towards compartmentalization strengthened by cultural mores of separation (social, political, religious—"them and us," as an example) serve to cement the brain into rigid thinking and the inability to respond and adapt to life's changes. Further down the road this lack of neural unity can lead to dysfunction, despair, depression, and even aberrant behaviors. From Hoffmann's perspective, the lack of psychological and neural integration plays an enormous role in all forms of personal and social dysfunction. She adds, "It becomes clear there is much internal work to be done if we are to successfully transform our neural pieces into a unified and whole interactive system that helps us achieve our goals of happiness, wisdom, creativity, and love."[4] Because the brain cannot complete this process left to its own devices, we are required, with our awareness or mind, to engage in a process of intentionally laying the groundwork for new neural pathways, modifying the old ones, and letting go of those actions and beliefs that are no longer useful. Hoffmann eloquently describes this process by saying: "Neurogenesis is stimulated by the perception and recognition of the activities of the inner world and how they interact with activities in the outer world: the personal and social dimensions of intelligence. This neural integration occurs through potentials that we commonly refer to as intuition, insight, foresight, and awareness by which we gather information using light."[5] She goes on to add that, "Self-awareness is synonymous with brain awareness and leads to neural integration. It includes many activities and potentials based on one function: seeing inward, the function of insight. Quantum scientists have proved that their mere observation of photons changes their direction. The same principle applies to the brain. Self-observation and self-examination can change the direction of neural connections."[6]

Neuroscientist Elkhonon Goldberg, in *The Executive Brain: Frontal Lobes and the Civilized Mind*, identifies the frontal lobes as the region in the brain associated with intentionality. Hoffmann adds to this concept by suggesting that the frontal lobes, the most recent evolutionary brain development, offer us a radically different identity, one that is of a spiritual nature. "Further, this new potential is based on the behavior of energy, not mass, much of which is held, like a womb, in the dark fertile possibility of intentionality. Similarly, because we are finally recognizing that the behavior of energy is full of possibilities instead of certainties, we have realized that quantum and chaos theories are unrelated to Newtonian physics."[7] This points us back to Rollo May's notion of intentionality and will in our earlier discussion in Chapter 1. Our ability to imagine or envision directly affects in a quantum way what we create in the outer world.

HARNESSING THE POWER OF THE NEUROPLASTIC BRAIN

Returning to the topic of musicians, it is not uncommon for artists to be held back from igniting the frontal lobes toward a process of change and integration, and a continual process of adaptation and flexibility. In our culture, the neocortex and to some extent the limbic system rule, driving our focus on survival, false power, fame, emotionality, impulsivity, and so forth. Wagner's epic *Ring* cycle deals with this powerful archetypal theme: choose power over love, all in twenty-some hours. The consequence of this choice needs no explanation—certainly if you are familiar with the *Ring of the Nibelungen*. Goethe also informed us of the consequences when we make those "Faustian deals."

Although survival needs are important, they cannot be at the expense of wholeness. Whatever we choose, however, the brain will respond to the repetition of those choices. I often warn my students that the brain is by nature "amoral." Be careful what you practice because whatever is done in a repetitive fashion, whether it is a belief system or a physical action (like bad fingering!), will have an accompanying neural pathway. Be careful what you ask for.

Beyond these concrete applications of brain plasticity, we can go further to embrace the transformative experience, connecting to what Jung refers to as the "numinous." This term was first used by Rudolf Otto in his work *The Idea of the Holy*. It refers to that nonrational experience of the mysterious divine, something greater than ourselves outside quantifiable comprehension. In Oliver Sacks's *Musicophilia: Tales of Music and the Brain*, we are reminded of how the numinous experience can work: "Music, uniquely among the arts, is both completely abstract and profoundly emotional. It has no power to represent anything particular or external, but it has a unique power to express inner states or feelings. Music can pierce the heart directly; it needs no mediation. One does not have to know anything about Dido and Aeneas to be moved by her lament for him; anyone who has ever lost someone knows what Dido is expressing. And there is, finally, a deep and mysterious paradox here, for while such music makes one experience pain and grief more intensely, it brings solace and consolation at the same time."[8] The experience that Sacks describes can provide an expansion of one's sense of aliveness and a glimpse of the eternal, as well as a kind of catharsis.

Musicians are regularly in touch with and, I dare say, invite the numinous experience. When we understand transcendence we recognize the cosmic pattern. Returning to Hoffmann's thesis, "The pattern of wholeness is a universal constant and creates in the mind that understands it an awareness of cosmic organization. Such a mind leaps the boundaries of cultural perspective and begins to understand the nature of the cosmos. Such knowledge is neither humanly nor culturally based. It is a *recognition* of a cosmic pattern. That recognition has been termed *transcendence*."[9]

But what does all of this brain science actually have to do with career development? By understanding how the brain functions, its neuroplastic properties, and how we might through the mind engage our whole brain, we can find our way to live holistic and transformative lives. This is the central foundation for developing an artistic vision and consequently crafting a concrete plan to realize that vision. It literally takes the whole brain. By engaging the whole brain in an ongoing and flexible process, an artist can readily respond to both changing internal circumstances and the morphing external "sordid market place." We find new solutions to the vicissitudes encountered on our artist journey, we deftly dodge the traditional vagaries of the music industry, and we come to understand that we are in charge of our careers, discovering how to thrive.

So how do we ignite the neuroplastic possibilities of the brain? Certainly significant external events can sculpt dramatic responses from the brain. I believe, however, that a more positive and proactive genesis for engaging the whole brain can begin with desire—desire for change, wholeness, something new, a project or vision that calls to us. The mind, or what psychologists call the "observer self," engages the flexible brain to make changes—creating new ruts in the brain, new actions and thoughts that are practiced. This could include new physical responses to playing our instrument. Other examples might include the exploration of somatic awareness through such models as the Feldenkrais Method or the Alexander Technique. We might choose to examine measured responses at the emotional level (not being trapped in the limbic system) or simply change a belief system (for instance, letting go of the false notion there are very few jobs for musicians). These concepts can all speak to this process of the mind directing the brain.

DESIRE AS THE GENESIS FOR CHANGE

The genesis for change stems from human desire. This element of desire, however, comes from deep within us. That source of desire is identified by many as the soul. There are others terms for this source as well: higher self, greater self, divine spark, and so on. James Jordan refers to this inexhaustible source as one's "center."

> One's center is the internal focus of one's being. It is the place where the experiences of one's entire life reside, but are not compacted or pushed down. Those life events both happy and sad are the place from which truthful music grows and is nurtured. Center is also the place where one's profound life beliefs reside. Beliefs in faith, others, and self all occupy this very sacred place. That place is a wellspring of energy and life that gives music its sinew and core. Center is the place by which you stay both connected to the ground and the earth, and to the world around you. Your center provides stability and strength. It provides the kindling for trust in self and trust of others. Most importantly, one's center is the place from which human love, care, humbleness, selflessness and giving flow.[10]

This center or place of the soul is the source of creativity. The imagination resides there along with our desires and visions of an integrated life. Abraham Joshua Heschel in *God in Search of Man*, writes that: "All creative thinking comes out of an encounter with the unknown. We do not embark upon an investigation of what is definitely known, unless we suddenly discover that what we have long regarded as known is actually an enigma. Thus the mind must move beyond its shell of knowledge in order to sense that which drives us toward knowledge. It is when we begin to comprehend or to assimilate and to adjust reality to our thought that the mind returns to itself."[11]

As artists we know this place and we visit it often. Our soul is the source of the infinite, the imagination, wisdom, love, empathy, compassion, and joy. The soul knows our deepest needs and if we are listening, it will tell us where to go. Gary Zukav, bestselling author, physicist, and philosopher, in his award-winning book *The Seat of the Soul*, describes it in the following manner: "It is the health of the soul that is the true purpose of the human experience. Everything serves that."[12] He goes on to conclude that: "Rather than a soul in a body, become a body in a soul. Reach for your soul. Reach even farther. The impulse of creation and power authentic—the hourglass point between energy and matter: that is the seat of the soul. What does it mean to touch that place?"[13]

This then is the guiding principle for the mind to engage the plasticity of the brain. Through self-awareness we take the knowledge of the soul or place of center, that which represents our deepest creative desires, that which moves us forward in new and innovative ways and supports our being as authentic, life-affirming, whole, generative, connected with both the internal and the external worlds, and above all creative. Desire is the engine that can fuel our transformation. It propels the mind to answer the call of the soul and to direct the mind in working with the neuro-plasticity of the brain. The mind can serve to organize or channel psychic material. The mind can also observe the body's wisdom. Somatic awareness can provide deep meaning and satisfaction as well. From this awareness, the mind can create new superstructures that the brain begins to practice.

Returning to Hoffmann's insights, she adds, "In forming an allegiance with the frontal lobes' agenda of integration, we initiate the germination of new neurons, synapses and neuro-chemistries in our brain that eventually connect all the other cortexes, creating wholeness. Only by creating this wholeness—which eventually disarms the egoistic, denial, and dominance apparatus in the brain—will we be able to overcome the immense obstacles to be faced in the future."[14] This process is life itself. From birth to death we follow this spiral journey from the soul's desire, to the mind, then to the brain, ever deepening our humanity.

When we come to understand our soul's deepest desire for expression and the riches of the neuroplasticity of the brain, we are ready to create our own dynamic musical career, adapting to change, fostering innovation, ever present to our inner and outer circumstances. Knowing this, we are now ready to create our own personal artistic vision and craft a plan to realize that dream. We begin to thrive as artists in the world, uplifting humanity, bringing into present time the numinous experience of music.

Your vision will become clear only when you look
into your heart.
Who looks outside, dreams. Who looks inside,
awakens.
—CARL JUNG

5

CREATING YOUR VISION

THE QUEST FOR A VISION

Writing about how we develop our own personal artistic vision can at times be challenging because it is not a fixed or prescribed process. As an artist, I am fully aware of how I heed the call of my soul's desire, the trips and turns I make, the doubt and resistance I must overcome, and the faith upon which I must rely. But like all artists, my way is unique. As the fourteenth-century guide to the spiritual experience *The Cloud of Unknowing* expresses it, "a man engaged in this work should not consider another worker to have the same experiences as he himself has."[1]

There are literally an infinite number of ways to discover your vision, and artists create a myriad of strategies to realize what works, what inspires, and how they can begin crafting a plan coherent with their artistic dreams. To describe a specific way that we create our vision or to present some sort of all-encompassing prescription is impossible. There is no one generic path for the creative process.

An artist might discover that there are varying nuances to how one creates that personal vision. Some begin with just a sketch or impression of what they want, others respond out of a growing sense of dissatisfaction, while others must free a dream that is buried deep within the subconscious. The quest for a vision is the soul's journey to self-actualization. There are many paths one can take for this journey, and for most artists, this process is repeated time and again throughout life.

Creating your personal artistic vision can sometimes feel a little like the search for happiness. It's not something you can capture in a direct way. It's not something you put on your schedule for next Tuesday! You must create fertile ground from which emerge precious insights, those stories and dreams from the subconscious, and new connections between passion and practicality. There is much in the way of inspiration and wisdom, however, to be found in the world of myth and metaphor.

The ancient Greeks, for example, credited the nine Muses with inspiration, invention, and vision. These Olympian goddesses gave form and context to the creative act. The Greek poet Hesiod, in his epic poem *Theogony*, describing the origin and make-up of the Greek gods, first identified the Muses. Presiding over the arts and sciences, the Muses were a source that artists could tap into for help. Artists of all kinds felt a personal bond with the Muses, crediting them as the source of wisdom and inspiration.

As with many of their myths, the Greeks found a metaphorical expression for something intangible and, in fact, the archetype of the Muse still lives on today. Often we refer to "inviting the Muse" into a project, or searching for the Muse when our creative juices are running thin. In 1999, Hollywood released an amusing film on this very subject (*The Muse*) and took a hand in describing what might happen in contemporary times should a Muse decide to visit. Sarah, the Muse in question, does indeed help the protagonist, Steven Phillips, his wife, and children, as well as several of Phillips's screenwriter colleagues. Things go terribly awry, however, when Sarah decides to move into Steve's home and take over the lives of his entire family. The film is both witty and instructive. Looking for the source of our creativity outside oneself can be dangerous! Clinging to the Muse, as the film suggests, can also have dire consequences.

If, however, we look to the idea of a Muse within, then we have the opportunity to connect with powerful archetypes and deep sources of inspiration. As an archetypal symbol, the Muse allows us to get closer to an understanding of how inspiration and creativity work. We can identify with and relate to this feminine archetype, enlisting it in our process of envisioning. What are the qualities that the Muse brings to our creativity? How does the Muse serve to inspire and enlighten us to new realities and the soul's desire? The feminine archetype is the vessel for creation, it contains and nurtures the act of creation, and it is receptive, inclusive, eternal, and whole. Other images associated with the sacred feminine are birth and rebirth, gestation, fruition, the circle of life, and so forth. These images and symbols may find a place of recognition in an artist's endeavor and process. Like the Muse, our creativity cannot be "willed" or scheduled. We must create the right environment to invite the Muse and to connect with our own understanding of the soul's desire. The poet W. H. Auden expresses this beautifully in the concluding lines of his poem to the patron saint of music, "Hymn to St. Cecilia."

Blessed Cecilia, appear in visions
To all musicians, appear and inspire:
Translated Daughter, come down and startle
Composing mortals with immortal fire.

As we seek to create our own vision, these feminine archetypal images are the very qualities that are necessary. Later, we will incorporate the wisdom of the mature masculine archetype as we build the edifice of our plan. As artists we know that it is difficult to "drive" our work, and to superimpose a deadline for inspiration. Much like that search for happiness, it is an elusive quest. Instead, we are better off creating the fertile ground for creativity and inviting the Muse into our world. We can notice how we hold paradox, how linear timelines may not always be the best thing to focus on during the genesis of an artistic vision.

When we create a welcome home for the Muse, we move into the world of the archetypal feminine. The borders are fuzzy, the terrain fluid, and the cycle of rebirth central. We become what Jungian scholar Marion Woodman describes as the "butterfly"—that symbol of the human soul. In her groundbreaking work *The Pregnant Virgin: A Process of Psychological Transformation*, she suggests that:

> It is the twilight zone between past and future that is the precarious world of transformation within the chrysalis. Part of us is looking back, yearning for the magic we have lost; part is glad to say good-bye to our chaotic past; part looks ahead with whatever courage we can muster; part is excited by the changing potential; part sits stone-still not daring to look either way. Individuals who consciously accept the chrysalis… have accepted a life/death paradox, a paradox which returns in a different form at each new spiral of growth.[2]

Woodman beautifully describes that process of transformation and rebirth that artists experience repeatedly throughout their lives. Like the butterfly, we can emerge from our own chrysalis transformed in miraculous ways. Is it any wonder that artists can feel isolated, confused, or afraid, living in a society that does not speak this language and instead focuses on prestige, authoritarian power, fame, and fortune?

Artists can, however, rely on all kinds of internal and external sources. In *The Artist's Way: A Spiritual Path to Higher Creativity*, an insightful guide to the creative process, Julia Cameron identifies artists as visionaries—those who work to create a vision and bring it into present time.

> Artists routinely practice a form of faith, seeing clearly and moving toward a creative goal that shimmers in the distance—often visible to us, but invisible to those around us. Difficult as it is to remember, it is our work that creates the market, not the market that creates our work. Art is an act of faith, and we practice practicing it. Sometimes we are called on pilgrimages on its behalf and, like many pilgrims, we doubt the call even as we answer it. But answer we do.[3]

So in modern times we can find inspiration and energy from our own Muse. In a way it is calling forth what the Greeks knew to be essential; from the genesis to completion in any act of artistic creation. In modern-day terms, we can find in the Muse that embodied positive feminine archetype.

A number of explorers in the field of creativity can offer light to guide, our way. One well-known author on this subject matter is Abraham Maslow. In his book *The Farther Reaches of Human Nature,* he gives a vivid explanation of how certain behaviors can support our creative spirit.

> In the early stages of creativeness, you've got to be a bum, and you've got to be a Bohemian, you've got to be crazy. The "brainstorming" technique may help us toward a recipe for being creative as this comes from people who have already successfully been creative; they let themselves be like this in the early stages of thinking. They let themselves be completely uncritical. They allow all sorts of wild ideas to come into their heads. And in great bursts of emotion and enthusiasm, they may scribble out the poem or the formula or the mathematical solution or work up the theory, or design the experiment. Then and only then, do they become secondary, become more rational, more controlled, and more critical.[4]

Maslow hits the target because if you are critical or afraid in the early stages of envisioning, you may miss the good ideas, the ones that come slipping through from the subconscious, the ones that have been germinating out of your awareness while you have been tucked away as a chrysalis.

Oliver Sacks presents another take on this process. "We don't know about the genesis of creativity. While it may start with conscious, deliberate attention, things tend then to be forgotten, and get incubated, out of sight and inaccessibly, perhaps to emerge years later. And we don't know what's happening in those years underneath."[5] I like Sacks's exquisite description. It's a kind of gestation period—we are not really sure what the baby will look like...

So part of our work as artists is listening to the soul. Processes that can create room for this experience might include all types of what I call "indirect" activities—rituals, behaviors, or tasks that can create a space for the soul to be heard. Philosopher, musicologist, and theologian Thomas Moore offers much wisdom in his inspiring guidebook *Care of the Soul: A Guide for Cultivating Depth and Sacredness in Everyday Life.* In his innovative guide to living a more soul-filled life, Moore presents this valuable insight. "You can see already that care of the soul is quite different in scope from most modern notions of psychology and psychotherapy. It isn't about curing, fixing, changing, adjusting, or making healthy, and it isn't about some idea of perfection or even improvement. Rather, it remains patiently in the present, close to life as it presents itself day by day, and yet at the same time mindful of religion and spirituality."[6]

DISCOVER INSPIRATION: INVITING THE MUSE

Moore's insights speak to the wisdom of the soul and if we are to access this wellspring of knowledge, then it is crucial to find ways of inviting that soul wisdom and guidance into our lives—our own inner Muse. There are a number of ways to create fertile ground.

Retreat. To invite the Muse, a personal retreat can be a great place to begin, especially if you live in a metropolitan setting. Noise pollution, urban life, and digital devices (computer, phone, iPod, pager, ad infinitum) can distract us, and on occasion, provide unwanted stress. To quiet the mind, to have an experience of nonlinear time, there cannot be distraction. In fact, after many years of ruminating on the subject of this book, it wasn't until I went to the Oregon coast for two weeks that the book project began to take shape, becoming clear to me. I truly had a sense of it finally paying me a visit. For those two weeks I planned nothing; I included good food, a few things I had wanted to read (but of course had never had the time), and when the spirit moved me, I rented an occasional movie. My days were spent sleeping until I naturally awoke; I ate when I was hungry; I frequently visited my favorite bookstore, had special coffee, and walked for hours up and down the beach, rain or shine. The book project paid me a visit along with a Muse. There was no way I could have "made" this happen. I had to create an inviting environment for that process, and for me it required a change of scenery, a separation from the distractions of work, aloneness, and reconnecting with nonlinear time. As I mentioned at the opening of Chapter 3, "Chance favors the prepared mind." I had been preparing the book project for several years. What was needed was a visit by the Muse.

Therapist. Some musicians have found enormous support for their process by working with a gifted mentor or therapist. A wise witness can serve as a trustworthy mirror for your path and the choices you make. Working with a therapist does not imply a mental disorder. Actually, it is quite the opposite: seeking wisdom and having a willingness to learn new things is the mark of a healthy person.

Dreams. Dream work for some is a powerful tool in discovering the soul's desire. If you determine that you want to remember your dreams, then they begin to appear more vividly and regularly. Pen and paper at the bedside are essential. Again, finding the right counselor for this work is crucial. Some counselors are more equipped than others to serve as a guide in this realm.

Read. In reading what others have to say about the creative process, you will discover a treasure trove of materials that can become valuable resources for inspiration. In this book alone, I have endeavored to include an abundance of diverse authors as a way of revealing the wealth of information available. We can be greatly enriched by insightful minds, especially those who are out in front of us on the creative path.

Listening to other artists and the accounts they offer regarding their journeys also helps to validate my own. In their pioneering financial guide *Your Money or Your Life*, Joe Dominguez and Vicki Robin altered my life in a sudden and tangible way. I read this book and was forever changed by what the authors ask us to consider. If I didn't have to make a living, what would I do with my life? As I read the book, I started making a list of what I was currently doing and realized that very little of it was what I would do if I didn't have to make a living. The power of this realization eventually prompted my husband and me to sell our house, downsize, and prepare to buy a small cottage in France's Val de Loire. Our dream of living between two cultures was something that we had held close to our hearts. We had imagined that someday we would find a small *pied-à-terre* in a picturesque French village. That *someday* arrived serendipitously, much ahead of our linear schedule. One thing led to another and we began a music festival, joining Americans and the French in a cross-cultural institute geared to adult pianists looking for international continuing education. Dominguez and Robin's provocative ideas put me in touch with what I would be doing if I didn't *have* to make a living. I was overjoyed to find this inspirational book and to discover someone who could show the way. Reading gives me an instant group of kindred spirits who, like myself, may be exploring uncharted territory.

Journal. Journaling is also an excellent way to tease out desires and inspirations. Julia Cameron may be best known for her artful rituals of "morning pages" and the "artist date." She suggests that a regular use of these rituals can awaken your creativity. Briefly, they work this way. Morning pages are done in longhand, strictly stream-of-consciousness (write anything) and for three pages. These morning pages can diminish the ongoing censor in your mind and can move you to the other side of your fear, negativity, or even your moods. Because these pages are not "logical," we are moved into what Cameron calls "our artist brain." We leave our logic brain (or survival brain) behind. As we have seen in the previous chapter, the artist's brain is whole. It's the brain that is making new neural pathways and linking up the other brain centers; it thinks in paradox, nonlinear time, with an expanded consciousness. Morning pages can help us move to that space.

The artist date works in conjunction with morning pages. Cameron adds that, "In doing your morning pages, you are sending—notifying yourself and the universe of your dreams, dissatisfactions, hopes. Doing your artist date, you are receiving—opening yourself to insight, inspiration, guidance." That artist date is a block of time around a couple of hours a week, in which you spend time with yourself. It's a kind of personal date—no one else comes, a personal pamper time, solitude, perhaps play activity. It's the self-intimacy that my trip to the Oregon coast provided for me. It was fun, active and inactive, peaceful and exciting, and I allowed myself to nurture my creative spirit.

Another kind of journaling that is particularly useful during challenging times, those episodes in life that are shrouded in confusion, no clear sense of direction, perhaps two many external mandates, is to buy a beautiful, small, hardbound journal— one that fits easily into a briefcase or purse. When I work with this journaling model, I have it with me at all times and when an idea comes, I date it and record it. It doesn't matter what comes from this process, I don't assess or judge it. I am just gathering ideas and noticing my thoughts. I am mindful of being open to whatever comes. In time, my "idea book" fills with information. Sometimes among the pages, the Muse visits. In fact, this process proved to be a powerful catalyst for my first commercial recording.

Throughout my career and beginning with my first years of piano study, I have consistently been drawn to the music of contemporary composers. Like many professional pianists, I followed the traditional "conservatory" training, studying the masterworks found in Western European Art Music. While I cherish the gems in this body of music, my heart has always gravitated to the music that has been created since 1900. Early on, I had a nascent dream of performing and perhaps one day recording some of this music, particularly of underserved American composers. Given the opportunity, I regularly performed contemporary music, joined contemporary ensembles, and looked for new and exciting composers.

During my studies at the University of Washington I encountered one of the finest American composers of the twentieth century, William Bergsma. Bill had been head of the composition department at Juilliard but was eventually persuaded to chair the School of Music at the University of Washington. That's where I first met him. Over the course of many years, I studied with him, eventually becoming well acquainted with his extraordinary music.

When I began to put my recital program together for my New York debut, I knew immediately that I would include selections from his extended piano work *Tangents*. In *Tangents*, Bill was able to evoke an old-time vaudeville show. It would be just the thing for a debut recital! Bill gave me performance suggestions on the four selections from *Tangents* that I chose to include in the recital. It was truly a joyous experience to play the music that had captured my attention and passion and to work with a living composer, sharing his work with others. Again, my nascent dream emerged. How could I expand on this experience, one that so fully captivated my joy? The next steps were taken intuitively!

I asked Bill if I could work with him directly in preparation for a comprehensive recording of all of his piano music. Ironically, only a few of the *Tangents* had been recorded and in total his solo keyboard output was around seventy minutes of music— perfect for a commercial CD. He agreed to work with me and we approached Laurel

Records in Los Angeles to record and produce the CD. Since this label has been known for its high-quality recordings of contemporary music, I felt certain that this would be an excellent partnership. It proved to be that and more. Herschel Gilbert, president of Laurel Records, oversaw every detail of the recording, relishing Bergsma's fresh and innovative music. Bill's exquisite piano gems are now available on CD.

What started as a nascent vision, a kind of longing to delve into the music that vitally captured my imagination, gradually became a concrete goal. As my vision became clear, I put together the necessary plans to make the CD a reality. I was aided in serendipitous ways by organizations such as Steinway Pianos, Linfield College, the Oregon Arts Commission, and the National Endowment for the Arts. Herschel Gilbert went on to become a close friend and mentor. With Bill Bergsma I was indeed lucky to work side by side with a composer of real genius and to enter into an extraordinary dialog about the music on the page.

On many levels, the Bergsma recording project showed me how an inner-directed vision leads one in powerful ways. I had this dream of playing the music that spoke to me, I encountered a gifted composer, I saw the opportunity for collaboration, and the joy that came from this experience sustained me even when I wasn't quite sure how it was going to happen, let alone get funded. When I think about my career, the Bergsma project is the one that most deeply touches my heart. What touches the heart is an important compass for creating an artistic vision.

Mentors. Mentors can also serve as important guides along the way. These are usually professionals in the field who have been down the path of transformation and have a wealth of experience and wisdom. These individuals do not live out of the ego but from an authentic self and often have a natural gift for teaching. A fine mentor can sometimes shorten the planning process by offering real-world advice, validation for effective strategies, and encouragement when the going gets tough. Often they can assist with the brainstorming process that is so crucial to creating an artistic vision, reinforcing a nonlinear course of action that invites the Muse. Those mentors are like diamonds: rare, beautiful, strong, reflective, and precious.

Friends. As artists, we are also social creatures in community with others. By finding one or two truly authentic friends who value the musician's journey, we can learn much. This two-way partnership can offer wise counsel, honest feedback, validation, and support. Doing this soul work is difficult if not impossible in a vacuum. Having supportive friends on the vision path is essential.

Bodywork. One's soul energy and the life of the body are not polarized opposites, and in fact most musicians come to understand experientially that we are our bodies. In making music, an artist uses the entire body, or in the case of singers, the instrument is the body. Most musicians are closely in touch with the physical presence of the body. Nevertheless, we live in a culture that has, until recently, worshipped the mind—I think therefore I am (Déscartes). Writing on the subject of somatic aware-ness, Stanley Keleman, in *Somatic Reality: Bodily Experience and Emotional Truth*, describes succinctly the wisdom of the body. He offers this keen insight:

> The notion of energy, as elucidated by Bergson and Freud, led me to pursue the experience that could help me know myself, my world, the nature of living, and to arrive at a path that was satisfying and purposeful. In pursuing this energetic psychological direction I worked with my own body in an attempt to uncover the unconscious and to experience the *élan* directly. Whether I chose to use my mind to observe or free associate, or to use my body as an attempt to intensify my excitement through breathing, or to do exercise meant to loosen the sociological muscle contractions, I was led to a deeper and surprising knowledge of my body. I found that both an intensifying of feeling and image making was a result of these explorations. I began to have a whole range of experiences, which encompassed past and present, ideas and needs, thinking and feeling, urges to act and urges to wait, archetypal pictures and emotions, inner and outer space and time.[7]

From this somatic work, Keleman experienced his own personal epiphany. He had found his own *élan vital* and had discovered that it presented a continuum of experiences that "had a tending, a predictability, an urge toward form, toward forming."[8] This discov-ery brought into stark relief the illusion that the body was separate and inferior from the mind. William Blake knew this when he said: "Man has no Body distinct from his Soul." Keleman understood that the somatic process is actually more inclusive and com-plex than what has been generally held to be true. It may be useful to briefly summarize not only Keleman's thesis but also those of several other leading somatic approaches.

Keleman posits that how we have accumulated information and experience shapes us as human beings, and the process by which this occurs becomes the secret to how we help ourselves grow. He suggests that there are three distinct stages of experi-ence that life changes contain: endings, middle ground, and the stage of formation. Accordingly, each transition requires a period of separating, a time of waiting, and a time for reorganizing new action. For Keleman, "Transitions are acts of imagination and image formation. They are acts of freedom, individuality, and self-regulation which can teach participation in the body's changes. They speak of our ability to respond and be sensitive to new patterns, shapes and form."[9] This is at the heart of a continuing lifelong response to the soul's desire. We are forever changing and morphing into an ever-expanding self. By understanding our own somatic reality more fully, experienc-ing each life transition, we are able to enter into a visioning process that can fulfill the nature of our individuality, our gifts, and our service to the larger collective.

The Feldenkrais Method, a leading approach to somatic education, devised by physicist and judo practitioner Moshe Feldenkrais, teaches through movement a means of functioning well that includes the ability to have access to a full range of responses to any situation. Identified as "awareness through movement," the Feldenkrais Method is an approach to body/mind exploration that offers individuals, through experiential learning, a path to greater flexibility, thereby creating new possibilities for dynamic living. This form of self-education focuses on developing the mind/body awareness, as opposed to manipulative therapy.

There is, of course, a rich panoply of methodologies for bodywork. Many musicians have explored such areas as: the Alexander Technique; various disciplines including yoga, Rolfing, Shiatsu; and movement or dance traditions such as Ta Chi or Qi Gong. Artists have found additional support in meditation practices, spiritual work, and even a clearing and purging of one's physical environment, setting things into a favorable *Feng Shui.*

All of the above modalities can serve to open you to a fertile envisioning process. Finding new ways of being, new thoughts and dreams, and opening the channel to the soul's desire are possible through this work.

As you begin to envision your career path, it is essential to cast aside false beliefs about the music industry, eliminating negative self-talk and being meticulous about what is true. Back to the Greeks: "Know thyself" (Socrates). It is, however, equally important to take Oscar Wilde's sage and witty advice: "Be yourself, everyone else is taken." You may find yourself on the razor's edge: making an honest assessment of your talents and strengths while being open to countless possibilities. Great art often holds a paradox and crafting your vision is certainly no different. Sometimes one must simply move forward, and in the face of fear. For artists, fear can be the single biggest crippling agent.

KNOWING AND FACING YOUR FEARS

Any book on music career development must inevitably address the topic of fear. As musicians, we must face the music so to speak about the inner demons that hold us back, trap us in small corners of the brain, and prevent us from living lives of fulfillment and service. Fear prevents us from being whole. Fear can hijack our envisioning process.

"We have nothing to fear but fear itself" (Franklin Delano Roosevelt). "We have met the enemy and he is us" (Walt Kelly from his cartoon *Pogo*). These sayings are more than slogans. They speak to a deep place within each human being that can respond out of fear. Or perhaps "react" is a better term.

Back to the brain. Fear is a kind of hyperarousal, which is mediated by the limbic system. It regulates survival behaviors and emotional expression and plays a central role in memory processing. Additionally, the limbic system affects the autonomic nervous system, which in turn regulates smooth muscles such as the heart, lungs, kidneys, and so on. From the limbic system there are two branches: the sympathetic and parasympathetic. Ideally, at least most of the time, these two parts are balanced.

Under extreme traumatic threat, the limbic system responds by pumping into the body a host of hormones that prepare it for defensive action. Depending upon a number of factors, such as likelihood of survival or the timeline of the threat, the body moves into one of three response modes: fight, flight, or freeze. These responses are not cognitive but rather, reflexive.

For those individuals who have been subjected to chronic high fear arousal, the brain can move from a normal healthy response to fear to what scientists refer to as "post-traumatic stress disorder" (PTSD). Even though the threat has passed or has even been survived, the body continues to respond as though it were under threat. In her article "Post-traumatic Stress Disorder: Identification and Diagnosis," Babette Rothschild offers the following description of how fear can work within the brain.

> During traumatic threat, it has been shown, that the hippocampus becomes suppressed. Its usual function of placing a memory into the past is not active. The traumatic event is prevented from becoming a memory in the past, causing it to seem to float in time, often invading the present. It is this mechanism that is behind the aforementioned PTSD symptom of "flashback"—episodes of reliving the trauma.[10]

Most people have not suffered from the effects of extreme fear or threat of danger that result in PTSD. Fear comes in many flavors, however, from something mild such as taking a chance as a musician in trying new repertoire to bolder concepts in the realm of public performance and performance anxiety. Fear can also hold us back from answering the deep desires of the soul. Stanley Keleman speaks eloquently about the relationship between desire and fear.

> Like reason, desire is a process, maturing and changing shape and expression, that can be educated. Unfortunately, the culture has seen neither love nor desire as a process. To be able to see them in this way resolves the artificial duality between love and reason, between individuality and community, and establishes a groundwork for desire, feeling, and love to evolve their own process of expression from which reason grows. Because we have not been educated in how to form our changing needs and desires, we come to regard with fear the natural impetus to transform ourselves and our relationships; with a lack of understanding of the formative process, we attempt to fix ourselves, to prevent change from occurring. We often develop lifestyles which make us prisoners of old needs rather than risking development and expansion.[11]

There it is: fear holding us back from "development and expansion." If we think about a fear-based belief system as something that can be lived over and over again, then it stands to reason that the brain develops those little "ruts" which reinforce arcane convictions and behaviors. The mind, however, our observer self, can thankfully intervene. As I discussed in the last chapter, one can redirect the brain, creating new neural pathways.

When we begin to consider our vision as an expression of our soul's deepest desire, we are often derailed by negative information that has no basis in truth. Sometimes this can be in the form of an inaccurate assessment of our skills and talents. I like to encourage musicians who are beginning this process to look objectively at their previous successes. What has worked in the past? What has been your finest hour? What were the circumstances that led to your exceptional accomplishments? What have your trusted teachers offered you in the way of feedback and advice? In what do you excel? What gives you the greatest pleasure and joy?

It's easy for us to compare ourselves with others who we find are more successful, talented, skilled, clever, or just plain lucky. This process of outer referencing ourselves is one of the biggest negative distractions, often preventing our professional success. We can end up measuring ourselves against others, searching for what they have, or who they are, and miss our own greatness. There is plenty of work to be done in developing one's career. It is best done on ourselves.

Even as we assess ourselves, there are many false beliefs that abound within the music industry. Here is my list of ten powerful false statements to which many, I find, subscribe.

 EXAMPLE 5.1

TEN SHOWSTOPPERS

1. I didn't win the Van Cliburn Competition (actually I've never won anything) so I will find it next to impossible to have a career.
2. I am too old. If I haven't done it by thirty, forget it.
3. I didn't go to a conservatory or well-known school and will therefore have few opportunities available.
4. I don't have enough repertoire, concertos, sonatas,... (fill in the blank).
5. The repertoire that interests me will never have a market.
6. There are too many pianists (or whatever) already.
7. I can't do that because other professionals aren't able to do it or haven't done it.
8. It will take forever to develop my career and it is probably too risky anyway.
9. There's no place for me because the market is already saturated.
10. I can't have a career without management.

Think of all the professional musicians you know who have in some way succeeded in spite of these tiresome caveats. In fact, these "showstoppers" can apply across the wide spectrum of professions in the music industry. These false mandates are simply distractions without grounding in any credible data. Or as my mother would say, "Just because someone says it, doesn't make it true." Still good advice!

The outer world can also present what I consider one of the most destructive impediments to artists: trusted teachers or "experts" who unilaterally decide whether you can or cannot realize your vision. I have been shocked and angered by the abundance of stories from clients and colleagues that describe judgmental, negative, and small-minded teachers handing out destructive as well as incorrect information about how the music industry functions.

One artist I know had dreams of creating annual salon recitals, featuring composers from a particular country. She would provide lecture–performances and research every detail, to include the correct food and costume, and even what poetry might be read. These salons, true to form, would be featured in the homes of friends. While in college, she had been told by her major professor not to consider a career that would include performance; that she would be disappointed and hurt by the fact that there was just too much competition and that she did not play well enough. This was, interestingly enough, after she had paid for four years of undergraduate work as a music major in piano performance.

Nevertheless, she moved forward with her dream. The first thing she had to do was recapture her vision and to take a bolder, more strategic look at how she could realize her innovative ideas. She went on to thrive in her dream of sharing music *her* way because she reconnected with what she really wanted to do. Her desire and passion provided the necessary compass. For her programs, she chose works that truly spoke to her interests. Her enthusiasm for these works inspired her to prepare the music to the highest level, committing to many hours of preparation, seeking input from master teachers, and researching important details of each composer. From there she made her plan as to *how* she would put the programs together in the most polished and professional manner. Not only did she enrich the lives of many, but also her work gradually expanded to include working with nonprofits through her salon-style performances.

In considering the notion of one's vision, I return to Dominguez and Robin's earlier question about what you would do if you didn't have to earn a living. This question allows you to get to the heart of your vision because it removes you from the distraction of earning a living and all the mandates, rules, policies, and orders that can stem from the left brain. In fact, it may be the most enticing invitation to the Muse. This question can put you directly in touch with your passion for music and your soul's desire. It can also sidestep fear. If you were completely free from financial pressures and responsibilities, how would you want to live your life as an artist? What would be your contribution to the world? In focusing on this question, you can get to the heart of what you truly envision. Developing your income remains a separate endeavor and solving the challenge of income production may or may not intersect with your work as a musician.

Albert Einstein said that imagination is more important than knowledge. One's vision comes from the land of imagination. It reflects your notion of what you are uniquely qualified to do. This has to do with your passion, your commitment to that passion, talent and skill, and knowing who and what you are. Some people have little practice in the blurry, watery, feminine world of imagination and dreams. Like the light of the moon, things are reflected from other sources, boundaries are unclear, it may be twilight and images are fuzzy. Many of us feel safe when we have a sense of control, security, and predictability. Truthfully, however, like the emperor's new clothes, these don't actually exist. Like that edgy fairytale, however, many people will talk about control, security, and predictability as if these are somehow concrete issues. To pretend that they are real can give to some a fleeting sense of calm, a way of medicating their fear, at least keeping it at bay. Don't listen! To chase after these illusory things is to truly leave the path of the artist, squandering energy, subscribing to false information, and chasing the proverbial windmills. This kind of distraction robs you of your valuable energy and time that are needed in developing your own career.

Working with our fear is the key to diminishing its power over us. In working with fear on a daily basis, either with clients, students, or myself, I devised six prescriptions that I find can assist in lessening fear's grip.

1. I know that it is unlikely that I will simply banish fear out of willpower. Rather, I must paradoxically accept it but give it a seat on the back of the bus. I like this image because in grade school if you were in the back of the bus, it was chaos. You couldn't hear anyone. It was pandemonium. Meanwhile, however, I am metaphorically sitting in the front, driving my own bus, deciding where I am going, ignoring the rabble in the back. Fear may be on my illusory bus but it has no role in determining where I am going nor does it have much of an audible voice.

2. "Act as if" is always a great place to start, creating new neuropathways of behavior. How would you behave if you weren't afraid? Ask yourself, what's the worst that could happen? Talking this over with a trusted confidant can be useful. Often I have ended the "how bad could it be?" conversation in laughter. In a way, by making peace with the unknown or what might go

awry, we can move forward with greater ease, having faced the fear of the worst-case scenario.

3. Don't knowingly terrify yourself. I often tell my students that they should feel slightly uncomfortable most of the time in my studio. They are being challenged, gently pushed forward into new territories, but I haven't thrust them over the edge into some metaphorical abyss. We can develop our courage "muscle" by continuing to do the things we most desire and in ways that are not traumatically frightening. For example, play a few regional concerts before your New York debut. Even a Broadway show has a preview in Philadelphia, Boston, or Baltimore before the Big Apple. It's about fear... and working with it.

4. The best antidote to fear may very well be routine. If you repeat something enough, the fear/anxiety quotient diminishes. What if you had to play your New York debut program every day at noon for your coworkers? At what point would it no longer produce anxiety? Day one, twenty, fifty-two, one hundred? At what point would your coworkers beg you to stop! Routine is the kiss of death to fear and that may be your best weapon.

5. Sometimes simply seeing and feeling your fear and going ahead and doing what you need to do anyway is a very simple solution. I advise my students who are experiencing performance anxiety to see if they can be so thoroughly prepared that even with the possibility that they will be afraid they will play well anyway. I find that it strengthens their preparation, they seek many preliminary performance opportunities before the "big" one (creating their own routines of performance), and we speak frankly about their fear and invent "back-up plans." Together we invite humor and storytelling as a way of remembering that it happens to everyone and that no one ever died (that I know of) when I played wrong notes or had a memory slip.

6. Lastly, talk to other professionals whom you trust about how they deal with their fear. One singer I knew had a technique that she swore by. Before a concert she went into a private room and screamed. I am sure it must have discharged enormous amounts of toxic energy. Just remembering her clever solution to performance anxiety puts me into a lighter place as I wait backstage. Another suggestion for useful imagery came from one of my teachers who recommended that his students imagine the entire audience as stark naked. Also very funny.

Whether you are facing a performance, job interview, public lecture, or even changing your career direction, it is crucial to bring fear to the table. By owning and inviting it into your process, you are considerably freer to move forward in your life as a creative artist. As the popular fairytale *Sleeping Beauty* reminds us, there are dire consequences when we don't invite the "bad fairy." For musicians, that bad fairy can often show up as fear.

One of my favorite authors, David Richo, in *The Power of Coincidence: How Life Shows Us What We Need to Know*, offers several tools for dealing with fear:

1. Sharing with those you trust who you really are.
2. Allow yourself to retreat from distressing issues long enough to regroup your strengths and return with a sense of personal power.
3. Pause to hold every feeling. Resist distraction and avoidance behaviors.
4. Face your fear: admit it, allow yourself to feel, and then act as if it were not able to stop or drive you.
5. With fear be careful to distinguish whether or not the fear is real in the sense of actual danger or pointing to something you don't actually want or are your fears simply obstacles to what you really want. You can usually tell the difference by looking at your own track record.
6. Are you carrying someone else's fear (a parent or spouse)? How is YOUR life different?[12]

How do we know when we are on the right track in our envisioning process? There are many indicators, such as a sense of awe, an awareness of effortlessness in our planning and response, synchronistic encounters that seem to strengthen our goals, and a joyful heart, to name just a few. More simply put, we discover that the positives in our life far outweigh the negatives. We find ourselves living from abundance, eager to take these gifts to the outer world. Rather than playing it safe and busying ourselves in our ongoing lives, we know that life calls us to expand over and over again and that there is no failure except in abandoning our own process.

I want to conclude this chapter on vision with what I think speaks best to the creative envisioning process. William Blake gives us the map: "The road to excess leads to the palace of wisdom." Here, I think that Blake was pointing to a deep and enriched engagement with life; plunging into the sensuous world where the spirit of things can be revealed—the realm of artists. Robert Johnson also speaks to this in *Ecstasy: Understanding the Psychology of Joy*, as he identifies the "Dionysian ecstasy that is filled with the profusion of nature's fruits, it is the divine realm, the garden of the gods."[13] Johnson and Blake are not referring to a world of material pleasure and depravity, where there is an infinite craving for more, but rather, they point us in the direction to the "palace of wisdom." That is our destination as artists if we have the courage to make that journey.

Once we have faced our fears and allowed our soul to express its deepest desire, we may discover that our vision is already in place—we know what we want! Sometimes, however, we may find ourselves at different points in the envisioning process—the continuum towards a concrete plan of action. Perhaps we have just a vague idea of something, perhaps our earlier dreams have been squelched by the outer world and must be carefully retrieved, or on occasion we are confused and unsure of what is best. The suggestions presented in this chapter are designed to provide guidance and inspiration for ways in which you can prepare the fertile ground from which your artistic vision can emerge. The search for an artistic vision is, however, a personal act of creation and discovery. Each person's method and process will be unique. In Chapter 9, you will find a sampling of true-life stories that present examples of the vision–plan continuum, offering what others have to say about their own journeys.

Lastly, there are ways of knowing that we are on the right track, that our vision is true, and that we are living in personal authenticity. In answering the following questions, you may find important validation to your emerging artistic vision.

 EXAMPLE 5.2

- If you didn't have to make a living, how would you choose to live out your vision?
- At the end of the day, does living out your vision leave you feeling alive and motivated?
- Are you excited to launch your vision even in the face of not knowing the outcome?
- Do you passionately want to share your vision with others?

If your vision is not clear, if you are still unsure about the direction you want to take with your unfolding career, or if you are just plain confused, then try rereading this chapter! Plant yourself firmly in the narrative and see how it speaks to you.

Once we have created our inspired vision, knowing that in a sense it is our true calling, we can move to the next step and invite the mature masculine archetype to build the plan, create the edifice of our goals and projects, work with a timeline, connect to the outer physical word of putting a vision into present time. Once again, Blake offers us wise counsel: "We could say that desire without a distinct materialization is synonymous with unfulfillment." That is for the next chapter.

Now is no time to think of what you do not have.
Think of what you can do with what there is.
—*The Old Man and the Sea,*
ERNEST HEMINGWAY

6

FROM VISION TO PLAN

IN THE PREVIOUS chapters we explored how musicians can position themselves so they are ready for their own artistic vision. By responding to the soul's desire and working with the neuroplasticity of the brain, we come to understand that we can imagine new possibilities and we can bring forth those artistic visions in fresh and innovative ways, building on the past but designing for new and exciting futures. After we create a vision, then we are ready to draft the corresponding plan of action. As an artist, I am drawn to the work of the soul, but I am also a very practical person. I know that no vision, no matter how brilliant, can come into present time without a material plan of action. My mother use to say for just about any challenge or difficulty, "We just need to get organized." She was forever breaking down into very small tasks the goals that seemed insurmountable. A plan must be doable and concrete but, like any road map, it must be referenced to one's destination. In the case of musicians, that point of reference is their artistic vision.

I have divided the topic of creating a plan into two chapters. In this chapter you will find the key guiding principles that serve to create a dynamic plan of action. The discussion is centered on what you need to know before you create a business model, develop the necessary timelines, design your media and marketing materials, and access your professional advisers that will be critical to your success. In Chapter 7, the narrative turns to the specific nuts and bolts of your effective business strategy.

MUSIC PROFESSIONALS IN TODAY'S MARKET PLACE:
THE DYNAMIC ENTREPRENEUR

As music professionals, most of us have been trained to focus on *our* talents, *our* passions, *our* projects, *our* skills. Long years of rigorous training with countless auditions, lessons, workshops, advanced degrees, and of course hours of practice are necessary to bring musicians to the gateway of the profession. These are important and vital components to building our artistic vision. Today, however, our industry is faced with changing markets, challenging economic conditions, and rapidly shifting musical tastes and trends. Musicians must be ready to make paradigm shifts, responding swiftly and with increasing flexibility to the morphing market place. Like the famous British detective Sherlock Holmes, they need to look everywhere for clues as to where opportunity is.

The mistake that many artists make is that in an attempt to respond to changing markets they abandon their vision of who they are, what dreams and goals they cherish, and the unique qualities they possess to make the world a better place. The very qualities that define them can also serve to foster a thriving career. We most often find musical opportunities in the things that we do best, and that particular amalgam of talents and skills is what leads us to compete successfully in the market place. We become specialists in a way, living out our own unique musical blueprint. To measure oneself in terms of the success of others or the capricious fads found in the market place is to lose sight of what is truly marketable. As we are true to our own abilities and dreams, we attract others who are interested in those qualities. People who need our help are able to find us when we are living authentically.

Whether we are looking for a specific job, expanding our career activities, developing funding for a project, or widening our streams of income, the path to the goals remains the same: working as an entrepreneur. Seeing ourselves as entrepreneurs gives us a new paradigm as artists. We are at home with change, we can work dynamically with other professionals, and launch our vision into the world.

A music entrepreneur creates and sustains a viable career in the music industry. The goal here is to thrive. I avoid the word "success" in this context because it is a highly subjective word, emotionally charged for most, and does not account for the myriad ways that artists live. For some, success may be defined by living on Park Avenue, singing for the Metropolitan Opera. For others it may be heading up a music school for an underserved community. Others may measure success for themselves (and others) in purely financial terms. Music entrepreneurs, however, have several identifiable vital qualities:

 EXAMPLE 6.1

- They can think critically (whole brain).
- They enjoy problem-solving with imagination and originality.
- They experience passion for something in music and have made a sustained commitment to that passion.
- They are ready for change.

There is opportunity in every market. The key is to develop our careers and the income to sustain us while realizing that in whatever ways we choose to work, whatever the various jobs we have, they are not our career. For entrepreneurs, the idea of a "job" is simply a part of their larger career mandala. This is a critical concept since many musicians have been trained to seek one job as the defining point of their career. Paradoxically, you could have a single place of employment (a full-time job) but still hold it within the greater expanse of your career. Jobs, however, are never careers.

Most of us have oriented ourselves to first completing our professional training, usually involving long years in graduate school. Garnering concerts, recordings, publications, and countless credentials. We then set off to find that all-important job—perhaps being employed in a music ensemble or orchestra, landing artist management, acquiring a tenure-track job in academia, or fanning out into the music industry in such areas as recording, publishing, or arts administration. We hope that our first job may be the right job. We then set our goals towards anchoring that job—it can be in the form of vesting, tenure, multiyear contracts, and so on. We make sure all our professional activities are well documented and appropriate. Somewhere along this journey we hope to express ourselves creatively and to bring our gifts and talents to others. Often, however, that gets lost.

The time has come to change how musicians define themselves as professionals—not as employees who pursue occasional creative projects, who must have a singular job that is in their chosen discipline, but rather as entrepreneurs who work in the global market place. When we see our jobs as not the sum total of our career, we take the first step to freedom. Our career is much larger than any specific job. It is our personal artistic vision that becomes the touchstone of our efforts. How we choose to acquire income is secondary. Making a living and being an artist are two different activities. Sometimes they intersect, but not always.

VISION AND PLAN: THE INTERSECTION OF HEAVEN AND EARTH

In developing our careers, and as we engage in our formal training period, we need to also begin a lifelong process of being an entrepreneur. Early on, we want to enter into that vision–plan continuum and, as Welwood describes, join heaven and earth. Sometimes we can have a number of personal visions and the will to carry forward any one of those possible futures. Clarity and laser focus, however, are required in making a plan. No fuzzy ideas here. One artist I know, for example, explored her passion for both writing and music performance. Her challenge was to meld the two disciplines and to craft a new plan for herself. She also wanted to include her bilingual skills in Spanish with her interests in connecting with kids.

She was challenged by what she perceived as two mutually exclusive visions that were equally important to her. Her goal was to somehow integrate her passion for creating stories and narrative and the immediacy of live performance. Her outer world, with its more compartmentalized disciplines, did not reflect a dynamic synthesis of her passions. In the United States, however, we still look to professionals as primarily singularly focused. If someone asks you what you do and you say: "I am a concert pianist, a writer, a teacher, a career consultant, a mother, a wife, a friend, and a political activist," well, most people will wonder. We are a nation of specialists, experts who know more and more about less and less. This model does not serve the entrepreneur who must expand his/her skill set, think with the whole brain, and be ready for change and self-reinvention. Incidentally, that artist I spoke of went on to create a series of concerts and residencies tailor-made for young people. She regularly connects both public school children and members of their communities to diverse musical traditions.

CREATING THE PLAN: THE PATHWAY TO A DYNAMIC CAREER

The process of creating one's plan of action can derail even the most committed artist. It's where those ten false beliefs from Chapter 5 can distract us. We are often stumped about what to do next, and we may even have some fear and negative self-talk around whether or not it is actually possible to achieve our vision. This is where the next leg of our education begins. Just as most of us went to countless master classes, performances, and lessons to learn the intricate details of the concert repertoire, we must also discover new information regarding our careers; perhaps retooling and reinventing ourselves as musicians, doing our work in new ways. Acquiring new information may mean going to marketing workshops, business classes, some arts-management training, grant-writing conferences, or accounting classes. It may also mean that we periodically hire a specialist to help us with an aspect of our planning process.

As you begin the process of designing your plan of action, it is important to first find out who is interested in what you have to offer and who resonates with your vision. You will also need to design a schematic of that vision that will inspire and instruct. As you begin to craft your strategic plan, it will be essential to communicate what it is you do and how your overarching vision contributes to the market place. In that market place what is the need you are addressing? How does your work enhance the lives of others?

Bringing the notion of the *ordinary* into our lives as artists can also be helpful. When I speak about my own work I often say, "This is my job. It's what I do." Avoid putting your art on a pedestal. The notion of art as part of our everyday experience allows us to be relaxed, creative, poised, and imaginative. You can't brainstorm if you are feeling like a deer in the headlights.

Sometimes crafting our plan can seem like an overwhelming task, especially if we try to take on everything at once. Breaking down the process into several smaller tasks can be useful. You might adapt to your own process those initial questions I listed in Chapter 2 (for new clients). Below is an adaptation of that questionnaire from Chapter 2.

 EXAMPLE 6.2

- What are three heartfelt goals that are central to your work and who you are as an artist?
- How might you include these goals in a five-year plan?
- What do you see as the most obvious barrier to your success?
- What appears to be your most urgent and pressing professional need at this time?
- What do you find missing in your current strategy to achieve your goals (such as additional education, networking, funding, professional contacts, visibility, media coverage, and so on)?
- What kind of help do you need in creating a plan to realize your artistic vision?

Playing with these questions can often lead to self-discovery, clarity about priorities, and resources for a plan of action. These questions often reveal how, when, and where to launch a strategic plan. We all have intrinsic priorities that are most often hierarchical. For instance, I need some kind of income to sustain myself while I develop my artistic vision. That income may or may not be a job in music, interestingly enough. I know artists who have taken a half-time job with benefits that required very little of their time and energy so that they could devote themselves to their careers.

As I mentioned, being an artist and making a living are two separate activities. It is not necessary that they intersect to have an artistic career. Charles Ives is a vivid example of this stark separation between making a living and being a composer. By day, he worked as a successful insurance executive. This afforded him the freedom of working as a composer entirely on his own terms. One wonders what would have happened to him had he chosen a job in higher education.

Notice your own blocks to creativity, innovation, commitment, passion, and so on. I believe every human being seeks a life of vitality. When we are not living in that energy there is always a reason. In this case, knowing yourself is of great importance. Look also to the various kinds of intelligences that you exhibit. Where are your greatest strengths?

Howard Gardner, educator and psychologist, in his book *Frames of Mind: The Theory of Multiple Intelligences*, suggests that human beings display an array of different kinds of "intelligences" and that each person has an individual "cognitive profile." Gardner's thesis of various "intelligences" supports our subjective experience that we simply do some things better than others, that some skills are innate, that we hold special talents, and that we can both draw upon our excellence and work to develop those skills that may be latent. Gardner cautions us, however, by saying: "There is a universal human temptation to give credence to a word to which we have become attached, perhaps because it has helped us to understand a situation better.... [*I*]*ntelligence* is such a word; we use it so often that we have come to believe in its existence, as a genuine tangible, measurable entity, rather than as a convenient way of labeling some phenomena that may (but may well not) exist."[1]

For our purposes, I will subscribe to the idea that different intelligences do in fact exist, albeit in an intangible form. So, how do we measure musical intelligence? We know it when we see it, and we know it as well when it is not strong. Like emotion, it's difficult to quantify even though we know experientially that it is present.

We can look to Gardner's thesis as a way of marshaling those skills that we need in developing our career plan. Gardner identifies the following as the sum total of human "intelligences": linguistic, musical, logical/mathematical, spatial, bodily/kinesthetic, and personal (sense of self). What strikes me is that these six ways of perception/expression are all central to being a musician. Certainly we all have greater strengths in some areas than others. But what we know about musicians is that most begin study in childhood, and that playing an instrument well requires all of the above intelligences. So as musicians, we come to our career planning process with well-honed skills and an array of intelligences to draw upon.

Consciously changing our inner and outer language can also be a critical piece in allowing the plan to come forward. Deriving inspiration from models created by others can be useful in crafting our career plan. For example, drawing upon cross-cultural traditions, Angeles Arrien, cultural anthropologist and award-winning author, provides a richly designed four-fold way to bring our artistic visions into present time. Arrien coined the term "walking the mystical path with practical feet, the Four-Fold Way." She beautifully describes what musicians are called to do and also provides a schematic for how to design a responsive plan of action based on one's artistic vision.

The Four-Fold Way Program inspires "spirit in action" using cross-cultural components. The Four-Fold Way™ Program emphasizes four major principles that integrate ancient cultural wisdoms into contemporary life. The Way of the Warrior or Leader is to show up, or choose to be present. Being present allows us to access the human resources of power, presence, and communication. The Way of the Healer or Caretaker is to pay attention to what has heart and meaning. Paying attention opens us to the human resources of love, gratitude, acknowledgment, and validation. We express the way of the Healer through our attitudes and actions that maintain personal health and support the welfare of our environment. The Way of the Visionary or Creative Problem Solver is to tell the truth without blame or judgment. Truthfulness, authenticity, and integrity are keys to developing our vision and intuition. We express the way of the Visionary through personal creativity, goals, plans, and our ability to bring our life dreams and visions into the world. The Way of the Teacher or Counselor is to be open to outcome, not attached to outcome. Openness and non-attachment help us recover the human resources of wisdom and objectivity. We express the way of the Teacher through our constructive communication and informational skills. Leading, Healing, Visioning, and Teaching. Cross-culturally these four areas reflect the four human resources of Power, Love, Vision, and Wisdom. Most of us tend to over-express one area, while leaving the others underdeveloped. It is important to understand that these four ways are universal and available to all humankind, regardless of context, culture, structure, and practice.[2]

Each of these four directions can guide us on our journey and give us reminders about what is important and authentic. All journeys begin with "showing up." We are present to the tasks at hand. Paying attention to what has heart and meaning helps us eliminate the distractions of the outer world, centering on what is intrinsically important. Speaking the truth without blame or judgment puts us in touch with our true integrity and vision and helps us discover what is authentic in both our inner and our outer worlds. Being open to the outcome allows us to be flexible and creative, inviting synchronistic and serendipitous events to unfold as we put our plan into action.

THE PLAN VERSUS INCOME

Discussions of the vision–plan continuum can easily remain in the theoretical realm. For most musicians, the challenge of income production can be a serious stumbling block along the artist's path. Joe Dominguez, however, helps us realize that the vision or dream is never driven by having to make a living. It cannot be, otherwise we would end up being slaves to the changing market place rather than entrepreneurs deftly dancing with the evolving outer world. Nevertheless, most of us need income to sustain us so that we can be artists. So considering how we bring money to our efforts is crucial.

SOURCES OF INCOME

I believe that most of us work successfully in the arts not with one institutional job but by developing "streams of income." When we create multiple sources of income, it enables us to be more creative about where our livelihood comes from; it opens up more possibilities, enabling us to think outside the box. Sometimes being a music professional may include that "day job"—something to sustain you while you are putting together your artistic projects. Many artists, conversely, have chosen to go "on the road" and become masters of sales. Whatever choice you make in the area of income production, remember, as I have said, making a living and being an artist are two different pursuits. Sometimes they intersect but not always.

Considering those varied sources of income, I find that there are generally three paths that music entrepreneurs can follow, remembering that jobs are not careers but parts of the larger career mandala.

- Streams of income, internships, and volunteerism;
- A single job;
- Grant-writing and fundraising.

Before we launch into a discussion about each of these areas, the three have important commonalities. Searching for employment opportunities and other funding sources such as grants often begins with the Internet. Richard Bolles in *What Color is Your Parachute?* presents the *sine qua non* guide for job hunters. His companion website is a treasure trove of information for those seeking employment. Bolles's book and website are filled with helpful resources, résumé-writing tips, advice for designing an effective business model, information on how to start your own company or nonprofit, networking insights, and a host of other well-honed guidelines. His humor, straightforward writing style, and accessible language make this book an essential tool for any kind of job search. His companion website (http://www.jobhuntersbible.com/) is also regularly updated with ancillary support materials to the book. Bolles remains current, ready to respond swiftly should markets and trends change—a true entrepreneur.

For musicians, Angela Beeching's *Beyond Talent: Creating a Successful Career in Music,* now in its second edition, can provide excellent guidance as to where musicians can find jobs (areas of employment), general marketing and media tips, interview and audition advice, tips on managing your own performance work, and an excellent narrative that goes into great depth regarding a freelance career with gigs versus one type of job, such as in arts management or in a symphony orchestra. Beeching also touches briefly upon financial management, applying for grants, and everything from time management to dealing with the Internal Revenue Service. This is a superbly written guide for those working in the music industry. Along with Beeching's book, Nancy Uscher's *Your Own Way in Music: A Career and Resource Guide,* is also an inspiring resource for job hunters and those musicians who are exploring how they might wish to develop their artist plans. The appendices alone are well worth the book. They include information on the following: educational institutions, research for financial support, performance aids, assorted careers in music, the government and the arts, and international considerations.

If you have an interest in intersecting with the public or private school environment, then Bruce Taylor's *The Arts Equation: Forging a Vital Link between Performing Artists and Educators* is an essential resource. Taylor's brilliant narrative is a dynamic response to the long trajectory of funding cuts for K–12 music programs in the United States. For the music entrepreneur Taylor offers a wealth of material as to why we need to reengage our young people in music studies, how as entrepreneurs we can bridge the educational arena with the experiential learning that music offers, and how we can enrich our local communities with revitalizing this area of education. Taylor shows that by connecting educational institutions and performing arts organizations, educational benchmarks and standards could be met by local school districts while being mindful of budgetary limitations. The visiting artist, the school residency program, or performances on location are all ideas presented by Taylor. This artfully written book offers hands-on practical advice for how to bring the power of music to public school youth, connect with underserved communities, develop audiences from all walks of life, and find resources to support these and other music projects.

There are many excellent resources both online and in print media that are invaluable tools for the entrepreneur. That landscape is constantly changing. The bibliography for this book has additional suggestions. Once you begin working out the details of what you want to do, you can then look to more esoteric sources for additional advice. Some of those topics might include marketing strategies, consortia building, website construction, utilizing social networks, grant-writing, technology skills, accounting strategies, and program development.

Whatever your search may be, you will need throughout your entire professional life the overarching skill of networking. Networking is the alpha and omega of any career design or job search and certainly the cornerstone of a thriving musical career. I recommend that entrepreneurs begin their networking process with a list of at least fifty people. These networking contacts can be fellow professionals but may also include family, friends, relatives, former employers, teachers, and so on. For my networking list, anyone I know is fair game! From this list of fifty, you then request an informational interview. Ask for no more than twenty minutes and explain that this request is for professional advice as you begin your "search." I have found that most people love to give advice and if they don't think you are hitting them up for a job, then you are home free. Ideally, all interviews are in person but when distance is an issue, the phone or Skype can also work. I discourage email or social networks for this kind of personal connection since messages and contacts can be easily overlooked in the flood of information that most people receive on a daily basis.

I also caution my clients about the use of social networks available to date. In a *New York Times* article from August 20, 2009, Jenna Wortham's research regarding social networks provides a cautionary tale. "According to a study conducted by Harris Interactive for CareerBuilder.com, forty-five percent of employers questioned are using social networks to screen job candidates—more than double from a year earlier." You may want to review what you post, what you say, and what types of graphic images you choose. Still, there are important considerations regarding website development and social networks. Scott Kirsner, author of *What the Web Can Do for Your Career: Or Why We No Longer Need Agents, Publishers, or Flacks*, suggests that when artists offer something interesting, useful, or entertaining, then an Internet platform becomes an important resource for promoting their work and for connecting with global audiences. Certainly for all music entrepreneurs a personal website is an essential marketing tool.

From the networking list of fifty, one ideally gets two more names from each interview. You can do the math. In no time at all, the music entrepreneur has a list of some 150 contacts and has had numerous "practice" interviews, not to mention an abundance of new career information. Some contacts are inevitably blind alleys but by increasing the networking list, one increases the odds for employment opportunities. One should always have in hand for those interviews a beautifully written and printed hard copy of a résumé, business cards, and if possible a professional website already launched. I also favor rack cards since they are smaller than a brochure and offer more detail than a business card. It's the sort of thing you can hand someone in an impromptu moment. You never know whom you will encounter in your networking process. It's important to have digital and hard-copy resources alike. Moreover, employers will ask about these items if they have found you to be of interest to their organization. Lastly, always write (hand written) a thank-you note the evening of the interview and mail it the next day. You will be surprised at how many people miss this courtesy, and an additional chance to connect with a networking source.

JOBS: IS IT A JAY-OH-BE OR PART OF YOUR CAREER PATH?

Most of us need work that will provide financial sustenance, bread on the table, health insurance, and all the other monetary obligations that are part of adult life. There are an infinite number of possibilities as to how artists meet this challenge. Sometimes it does involve a bona fide single job in your career. That search may be an ongoing one that you attend to on a daily basis. At other times, pursuing multiple streams of income can be a wise choice, giving you more discretion over your time, and more independence (not answering to the contractual demands of one employer). It is quite possible to blend career work with those strictly "bread on the table" jobs. Sometimes those part-time jobs can be a low-stress ways of covering basic financial needs while avoiding time-consuming requirements such as meetings, retreats, after-hours projects, and assessment reports. Instead, artists can chose to strategically include vital internships or volunteer posts with an important professional organization, thereby strengthening their dossier while preserving valuable energy and time each day for their work as artists. Incidentally, when you volunteer your talents, you can choose exactly where you wish to develop key career contacts and experience. Those volunteer opportunities always have new networking connections, sometimes even leading to regular employment. When an opening appears, you are already on the ground floor doing a terrific job!

Whether you are creating a concert career, hunting for a specific job, or establishing something freelance, you need to identify and locate your market. One such innovative music professional who has created a thriving career for herself is Lauren Pelon. Lauren has appeared on *A Prairie Home Companion* and has toured throughout the world, appearing in television specials, and in programs throughout the United States, England, Ireland, Scotland, Canada, New Zealand, Australia, China, and Kazakhstan. As a humanities scholar and performing artist, she explores the story of music and instruments from antiquity to the present.

During the last twenty years Lauren has presented over 300 humanities programs with the support of numerous state humanities councils. In 1991, Pelon received the Utah Humanities Award of Merit for the music history programs she presented in Utah. In 1992, she was one of twelve ethnomusicologists and educators invited by the University of Michigan to tour the People's Republic of China and Kazakhstan in order to exchange ideas about the teaching and preservation of ethnic music and instruments. Lauren also gave the keynote address in 1995 for a conference on the history of European and Asian musical instruments at the Russian Institute of the History of Arts, St. Petersburg, Russia. She was the recipient of the 2001 Artist of the Year award from Southeastern Minnesota Arts Council, and received an Artist Initiative Fellowship from the Minnesota State Arts Board in 2010.

I have known Lauren for nearly thirty years and have had the pleasure of observing her exceptional work. In addition to being a gifted artist and a compelling storyteller, she is also an astute and capable entrepreneur. With over 100 performances a year, she is in high demand, enriching the communities she visits. Lauren books all her own tours and residencies, essentially functioning as her own manager; she funds many of her projects through her exceptional skills as a grant writer; she writes all of her musical arrangements, and is a composer in her own right. With her keen business acumen she is able to successfully juggle all these tasks.

Lauren is a model to other music professionals because she has a clear artistic vision and she is well versed in putting together a plan of action. She has found a niche no one else fills; singing and playing music she has composed or personally arranged on approximately twenty ancient and modern instruments. Concerts featuring these instruments and vocals have been her main source of income since 1979. Her clarity about what she wants to happen in her career enables her to respond swiftly to changing markets and shifting funding sources. Lauren has developed over a dozen different concert programs in response to the evolving needs of presenters and audiences alike. She has also found ways to supplement her concert fees with educational programs that fill out her concert tour schedule. Even here, as circumstances have changed, so has Lauren's approach. For example, as budgets were cut in school music programs in the late nineties, Lauren shifted her output, bringing a variety of music presentations to private as well as public schools throughout the United States.

More importantly, she knows how to connect with the needs of presenters and their locales. For example, Lauren frequently brings block bookings, educational resources, residency guides, and additional support dollars to her clients, often in the form of grants. She is able to provide local libraries, schools, and arts councils with information and materials for ongoing classroom activities long after she has left the community.

In the more recent economic downturn, with presenters making drastic cuts to their artist series, Lauren has offered help in the way of providing vibrant marketing pieces and strategies for the purpose of increased ticket sales for her performances, thereby insuring her return engagements. When Lauren goes into a community, she becomes part of that locale, stepping forward to bring music and story to life but also to assist with the challenges that community faces.

From her initial contact with a client, Lauren demonstrates why communities benefit from her services. She has neither an agent nor a manager but prefers to do all her own booking, publicity work, brochure design, and grant writing. And because she is able to multitask in so many areas, she can pass on the cost savings to her clients. Lauren Pelon is a success story and an inspiration to other music professionals. She knows how to match her artistic vision and plan of action with the right client, and this has enabled her to thrive as a performing artist and educator through fluctuating economic times.

My home state of Oregon offers another example of a potential client in need of a creative solution. The Oregon Department of Education has an elaborate list of benchmarks that all school districts in the state must meet. Meanwhile, we are experiencing devastating cuts to art and music instruction. The state of Oregon is rapidly approaching a situation that may even have legal consequences: districts not having the staff to fulfill the required benchmarks.

The fiscal challenge that Oregon faces is a virtual hologram for most states across the country. This financial squeeze, however, is ironically an opportunity for performing artists. School districts presently need arts specialists but cannot pay for enough permanent full-time teachers. Brief itinerant residencies given by artists have become a creative solution to this challenge. Additional support can also come from ticket sales to evening performances given by the resident artist for the general community audience. Other solutions might also be possible. The point is that an individual or organization with a great need can be a terrific opportunity for the innovative entrepreneur.

In the United States today, with the current stressed economic climate, there is a tremendous need for the arts. Those musicians will flourish who create self-sustaining solutions to educational arts benchmarks and who provide rich and attractive performance offerings to regional communities. One only needs to be reminded of Myra Hess's concerts during the London Blitz. Providing concert performances in a basement site of the National Gallery of London, Hess gave her audiences a sense of hope and normalcy as she and her musical colleagues defied the Blitz and "played on."

INTERNSHIPS AND VOLUNTEERISM: THE FAST TRACK TO
PROFESSIONAL EXPERIENCE

Two areas that can plunge you immediately into your chosen field are internships (paid and unpaid) and the world of volunteerism. Particularly if you have a brief work history, accessing one or both of these areas can quickly give you targeted experience in the career you have chosen. This is useful if you have a day job outside your career. Keeping your career goals alive with carefully chosen internships or volunteer posts will show your commitment to the profession, will give you valuable experience, and most importantly, these experiences can often lead to more permanent employment. Internships as well as volunteer work also serve as an ongoing source of networking with professionals in your field. A number of my clients have parlayed their internships or volunteer activities into contracted positions because they were there when something opened up, the employer observed what fine work they had done and what a positive team player they were. They clearly had a competitive edge over outside applicants. With both internships and volunteer work, the advantage that musicians have is that they can carefully target organizations, employers, individual mentors, or professional opportunities that are connected to their goals. It's the fast track to expanded networking in the area of the profession you are targeting and it gives you instant work experience with the possibility of developing that into a job. You can't lose!

GRANT WRITING AND THE WORLD OF PHILANTHROPY

For most musicians, the idea of asking for money for their professional projects or for ongoing support can be at times overwhelming, given the fact that there is some likelihood of rejection of their proposals. For some artists, it can also appear to be not worth the time. It's true, we are living in trying times and uncertain economic conditions. But as history shows, the boom and bust economic cycles occur as a natural ebb and flow of the free-market system. Economic circumstances, nonetheless, sculpt how we now search for funding support, requiring strategic, focused, and honest proposals. There is money out there for the arts and in fact billions of dollars in the government and nonprofit sectors. Becoming a skilled grant writer can amount to, literally, money in the bank. A number of things, however, have to be in place if you are going to succeed in landing the support needed for your projects.

There are excellent resources available to the musician new to grant writing. Finding a specific grant-writing workshop is often the best first step to plunging into this world of philanthropy, and most universities and colleges offer classes or seminars on this topic. Wherever you are in terms of your grant-writing interest and experience, I urge you to take a weekend workshop on this topic. Even for those who are experienced in this area, the landscape is continually changing. Being up to date on funders and their needs is crucial to finding support for your projects. For every grant writer, however, there are general principles that govern all successful proposals.

For the past few years I have worked as a performing arts adviser with John O'Malley, founder of O'Malley International Associates in Pasadena, California, a communications consultancy. John is also one of the finest proposal consultants in the United States and is a terrific resource for anyone looking to develop skills in proposal writing. In offering workshops and consulting to music professionals, I came up with the "Grant Checklist for Music Professionals—Just the Basics." Before you begin using this checklist, however, you will need an "artist's statement." For organizations seeking grant funding, this is the "mission statement." Each of these narratives is usually around 100 words and gives the reader a sense of who you are, your artistic vision, whom you help, and what you bring to society that is distinctive. Be prepared to persuade your reader as to why anyone should care about you or your work. You will also need a 400-word "project title and abstract" along with a clear and detailed budget. Lastly, you will need to have in place a consortium of preliminary funding, showing that there is already momentum in support for your work. Once you have these preparatory elements in place you are ready to use the "Grant Checklist for Music Professionals—Just the Basics."

 EXAMPLE 6.3

GRANT CHECKLIST FOR MUSIC PROFESSIONALS: JUST THE BASICS

I. Once you have designed your project, begin your online search for the right funding sources. You will apply to many. Connect with an institutional research librarian or your local college/university development office (you have resources as an alum!). They can assist you in your grant search. Be sure to have in hand your "mission/artist statement," "project title and summary," and a detailed budget before you begin the search. This will clarify your goals, your financial picture, and your project plan. You will need these items for most proposals.

II. Have additional support in place before you begin grant writing. If you have support in place, it is easier to get more support. In-kind contributions, cash donations, other grants, sponsors, underwriters, volunteers, and consortia: these are all sources that will enhance your grant proposal. It is crucial to build a consortium of support.

III. A good grant has:

A. An altruistic mission: making the world a better place. What is original and inspiring about your research or artistic project? How does it contribute to the mission of a foundation or funding agency?

B. Concrete evidence as to how *you* are the only one to make this happen

1. List your qualifications.

2. Provide a résumé written with an eye for the project and your target foundation.

(continued)

3. Offer professional media/publicity materials.
4. Demonstrate quality professional recordings, DVDs, etc.
5. Make available excellent references, letters of support, legal agreements or contracts, reviews, media coverage, accolades, etc.
6. Present a professional persona in correspondence, voice mail, email address, website, photos, stationery, interviews
7. Convey that the foundation/agency you are applying to is the tipping point for your project to happen. Co-opt the grantor into your project. Show that you already have evidence of other support.
8. Provide excellent writing skills. Familiarize yourself with the specifics of grant language. This is persuasive writing!
9. Follow two paths in seeking funding:
   a. As a nonprofit (you will need a 501c3 of your own) or you will need to write the grant under the umbrella of another nonprofit.
   b. As an individual for-profit organization (sometimes this may include an LLC). The NEA, state arts commissions, regional arts councils and the like often give under this umbrella.
10. Budget preparation: it must be realistic, clear, attainable, accountable, and fair. No charades. You may be audited.
11. Describe how this project will have lasting impact and for whom. Be clear about whom you serve.
12. In some cases, demonstrate how this project will continue to pay for itself. This is essential for any pilot program.
13. Write a superb grant report once you have completed your funded project. You may want to be funded again by that grantor.

Remember: Fill out the grant application exactly as it says. Provide all supporting materials exactly as requested, submit the grant on time and with return receipt mailing (if hard copies are used). Keep a hard copy of everything. Be meticulously neat and proof your work carefully.

As you begin moving through the checklist and you have developed an exciting, altruistic project that has lasting impact, and you have written a descriptive and persuasive project abstract along with the artist or mission statement, your attention will then turn to the budget. Before you develop your detailed (and defensible) budget, you first need to build a consortium of support that provides evidence regarding the resources you already have in place for your project. A consortium of partners that supports your project gives concrete evidence in your budget that there are already professionals on board with your ideas. Money attracts money. In a way, your project becomes "juried" by the support of other financial entities. It is much easier to attract support once there is a diverse and dynamic consortium in place for a project. Building a consortium for your project is the single most important component of a superb budget; it is also the gateway into creating a winning grant proposal.

Your consortium can have in-kind services (for example: free printing, donated office space, etc.), cash donations, underwriters for a specific item (providing a concert grand piano for a performance), volunteers who work on your project (their time is worth money), and even partners in fundraising events (sharing the proceeds with, for instance, a local nonprofit). There are an infinite number of ways to build project support through a consortium. Whatever you decide in terms of building your consortium, remember that it is an act of collaboration and networking. You are joining with others to bring a project to fruition. The most successful consortiums are those in which all partners benefit from the collaboration. As a successful grant writer you will be keenly aware of bringing together diverse partners to your project and demonstrating how your consortium will benefit all. In a dynamic consortium the sum is truly greater than the parts. You might even have fun along the way!

Remember, grant writing is something you can learn to do. It's not a special talent. If you have ever written a senior thesis or even the ubiquitous term paper, you already have the basic writing skills needed. What may be new to most musicians, however, is the style of persuasive writing that is required. You can learn this along with how to prepare a budget, build a consortium of support, and search out the most promising sources for funding.

PHANTOMS THAT DERAIL YOUR PROPOSALS

Even the best-intentioned grant writing efforts can be sabotaged by a number of thinking errors. Most artists are tightly connected to their projects; passionately attached to their success. Without prudent detachment, our projects can succumb to our own artistic narcissism. Here are several examples of self-interest running amuck.

1. My project is obviously great and so everyone will want to fund it. A foundation that understands my project will certainly want to give me money.
2. As an academic (this is particularly true for college and university professionals), someone else will write the grant proposal. Not me, it's not what I do. I am an artist, musician, (fill in the blank).
3. Foundation X is going to entirely fund my project.

It is easy to see the value of our projects when we spend so much of our creative time developing them. As artist/scholars, we are often bound to our projects at the emotional level. As musicians, we have spent nearly our entire lives acquiring professional proficiency—many hours of practice and dedication. We believe in our projects but often lack the necessary objectivity that is needed to write a winning grant proposal. The fact is that people outside your profession may read your proposal. Granted, they will most likely be what we call an "informed reader" but not necessarily someone who understands the keenest nuance of your professional work.

Instead, put forward your proposals as important vehicles for making the world a better place. Altruism is a central theme in all successful grant writing. Ultimately all grant writers need to answer these questions: Why should they (the funders) care enough about your project to give you (and not someone else) money? What is the difference *you* are making with your project? Does your project serve a large portion of the population? What are the lasting effects of your project long after it has concluded?

Most thriving artists are regularly creating sponsorships, producing successfully funded grant projects, and generating countless in-kind donations. In the United States alone, we have a tremendous financial resource that is indispensable for artists. It is the American public and their notion of the American dream. We all love the story of the underdog, the one who came from behind, the long shot. Our culture supports the rugged individualist, the one who takes risks and has courage. You are likely to get more help in our culture from foundations, individuals, and private agencies than from our traditional government institutions (NEA, local arts commissions, etc.). Compare the size of the thick hard copy of the Foundation Center's publication *Foundation Grants to Individuals*, to the thin pamphlet for the entire NEA program. There's about a 3-inch difference in thickness. There are countless funding sources that offer "matching funds" as well. In other words, if you can raise the seed money or the equivalent from in-kind contributions, you are in a strong position to attract those matching funds. You may even find that a number of sponsorships can provide start-up assistance as well as attracting other financial resources. Sometimes a professional exchange with another artist or arts organization can provide strong evidence of outside support. Individuals and foundations want to back a winning proposition and that is demonstrated by who is already contributing to your ideas and projects. Remember, building that dynamic consortium involves two essential skills: networking and collaboration.

Lastly, take that weekend grant-writing class. Through these workshops you can discover online resources, texts, and guidance that are essential in connecting to the global philanthropic world. You will also discover the secrets of effective persuasive writing and you will learn how to produce a realistic and defensible budget.

By periodically taking classes in this field, you remain current and avoid "reinventing the wheel." Moreover, you make new networking connections with other like-minded people.

YOUR PLAN: THE DEVIL IS IN THE DETAILS

In making a plan of action, it is important to continually ensure that your activities are rooted firmly in your vision. Avoid squandering your energy, time, or money on tangential seductions; something that seems like a quick success, a sure thing, or "easy money." If it sounds too good to be true, it probably is!

Most experts in business planning suggest that the average time for an enterprise to operate financially in the black is five years. Instead of looking for quick solutions, work from your strengths. Where do your various intelligences lay? What has succeeded in the past? What was your finest hour? These are moments that teach us about what we do effortlessly and where our true passion lies. These experiences also alert us to the right clients and opportunities.

TROIKA OF SUCCESS

There are three key elements that support any successful artistic plan. I call them the "troika of success." These essential components are:

1. Lifestyle;
2. A practical timeline;
3. Solid personal boundaries.

Each artist has a combination of nonnegotiable responsibilities; personal wants and needs, quality of life issues, locale preferences, and a host of other day-to-day considerations. How we put together our lifestyle can be crucial to the support of our vision. In other words, if I want a job with a major orchestra, I may need to consider moving from Nome, Alaska! If I want to go to graduate school, I may need to forgo the purchase of that BMW.

Along with personal considerations, your business model and timeline are essential tools in crafting your career plan. Referenced from your vision, the business model and accompanying timeline make it real. They keep you on track. You have a calendar of tasks to complete in a timely fashion—first one thing, then another. Without the business model and timeline we are less efficient and effective. It is the infrastructure of the overall plan and it reflects Arrien's measure of authenticity.

In the next chapter, we will look at how to build that dynamic business model from the ground up and create those realistic timelines that support it.

Whatever plan you craft, whatever timelines you construct, however, be on the lookout for serendipitous and synchronous opportunities. Sometimes you may build the road as you travel. In *The Power of Coincidence: How Life Shows Us What We Need to Know*, David Richo speaks to the power of synchronicity. He codifies what Jung suggested: there are no coincidences. Richo observes that synchronicity is ever present in our lives and that by understanding the richness of this reality we can discover support and direction for our career plans. Synchronicity, as described by Carl Jung, is "a noncausal but meaningful relationship between physical and psychic events.... A special instance of acausal orderedness.... Conscious succession becomes simultaneity.... Synchronicity takes the events in space and time as meaning more than mere change." The key word in this is "meaning." We are not stuck in linear time—instead, things can happen simultaneously.

One of my favorite examples of career serendipity involves a young man whom I will call Tim. One afternoon, Tim, an aspiring recent college graduate, was returning to Portland from Seattle on the train. As he glanced around the car, he noticed a man a few seats away practicing his American Sign Language skills. Since Tim had been studying this language as well, he decided to introduce himself to this young man. By the time the train pulled into Portland, the young man had offered Tim a job as a music editor in his publishing house. Tim, who was eager to express his interest in ASL, had intuitively reached out to this stranger. Tim was also in the process of searching for a job in the music industry. He was prepared for any opportunity including an interview, casual or otherwise, and he had on hand his résumé and business cards. The rest resides in the realm of synchronicity and serendipity.

Richo writes beautifully about this intangible notion that the world is interconnected. He offers a richly textured quantum view of reality.

There is a lifelong synchronicity in the link between our innate talents or gifts and our life work. Our talents bring us bliss when we follow them up with practice. When bliss and talent come together, we know what our vocation is and we find work that pays our salary. In addition, in our career we meet other people with inclinations and fascinations like our own and from among them come lifelong colleagues, friends, or partners. It all works together in a synchronous way so that who we always were makes who we are and will be one joyous and successful continuity. The synchronicity is complete when we feel grateful for the grace by which it all worked out and we feel a rise in spiritual consciousness.[3]

This is all by way of saying, pay attention. As you create your business model and timeline, moving forward in linear time, notice whom you encounter, notice what events occur in your life, notice how you feel both psychically and somatically about things, look for your own quantum connections. Careers are made from synchronicity and self-awareness. As we saw in the story about Tim, jobs can be found in the most unusual of circumstances. Yes, we do participate in making our business models, timelines, our five-year cycles, and the various tasks for each day, but much of what is crucial comes to us serendipitously. Pay attention. Synchronicity can connect you to your destiny (from the Latin "to determine" or act intentionally). It can also connect you sometimes quite simply to a job or financial support. Again, pay attention.

The last part of the troika involves our boundaries with others. As a pianist, teacher, consultant, mother, friend, wife, daughter, sister, and political activist, I can get lost in the demands of others. I am most effective when I am clear about a particular role and the reasonable time it deserves. Sometimes a "sabbatical" from nonessential activities is vital as you begin your planning process. Consider taking a break from extraneous volunteer work, hire help at home (a housekeeper, gardener, auto mechanic, etc.), and avoid individuals and institutions that usurp your valuable time and energy. Time and money are of equal value to the thriving artist. Sometimes we need more of one and less of the other. Keeping just the right balance between these two essentials is crucial.

The literature in career development does not often address this issue but intuitively most of us know that overscheduling, quick fixes, and the like can be damaging to artists and their endeavors. I believe it is the number one way we sabotage ourselves. It may appear that with so much hectic activity, our music careers are successful. To the outside observer, we are very busy. Our culture also tends to laud those who are operating 24:7. Last-minute concerts, workshops, presentations, and activities can be, however, seductive opportunities that may erode the time available for truly important work, diminish your preparation, and derail the many other important tasks on your schedule. Simply taking on too many projects can be disastrous. Many musicians sabotage themselves by overextending, and this lifestyle choice can often prevent them from performing to their full potential.

Lastly, avoid like the plague those people who are negative, jealous, or mean-spirited, and find that by bringing others down, they are somehow elevated. As Mark Twain suggested: "Keep away from people who try to belittle your ambitions. Small people always do that, but the really great make you feel that you too could become great." It is not unusual to hear from a disgruntled musician or even those watching from the sidelines that those who choose a career in music will simply succumb to being "a starving artist." If one buys into this grim view it is very helpful to have others confirm that perspective. Don't be that person. Along with the "Ten Showstoppers," these are words of discouragement full of negative energy with no grounding in the reality of how musicians can prosper.

SURVIVE OR THRIVE

There are two ways that we can exist in our careers, either by remaining in survival mode or by thriving. If I come from the perspective of abundance, if I understand that there is enough for all of us and I have faith in what I am doing, then I tend to schedule my time appropriately, according to my own particular needs. From this perspective, we are more likely to give ourselves time for our own health, for our practicing, preparation, and all manner of things that require our time. If we are insecure about our work and whether there will be enough, we set ourselves up for hardship, becoming stressed, distracted, and overworked. This can sometimes result in risks to our health. Certainly it is more difficult to offer our best work under those conditions.

Thriving conditions include understanding the importance of self-care. Many artists take better care of their cars than they do of themselves. Self-care includes, but is not limited to, a good diet, adequate exercise, sufficient sleep, spiritual renewal, a cadre of trustworthy friends, and the like.

As you move from survival to thriving, you are presented with choices everyday as to how best to use your professional time. I encourage you to choose wisely about each concert, workshop, or other professional commitment. I have three criteria that have proved useful in determining whether I should accept an invitation or opportunity that comes my way. Wherever you find yourself in the music industry, these can be useful evaluation tools.

1. A professional opportunity that generates a large sum of money in a short period of time. Most of the time I'll take this opportunity because it gives me some measure of financial freedom. Even if tangential to my career goals, it can in a short span of time provide maximum financial benefits.

2. A professional opportunity that will open a new door. For example, when I performed on the Dame Myra Hess Series in Chicago, the fee was quite modest. It was, however, a rich professional opportunity because, among other things, it was broadcast on 400 cable stations nationwide. Many new doors were open to me following that performance and I might even have done it for free!

3. This last example is a highly subjective one: something that is incredibly fun. This is a professional experience that gives unconditional joy and enrichment

to your life. The remuneration is of secondary importance and this kind of engagement may or may not necessarily open any new doors. You'll look back, however, and savor it for years to come.

Being mindful about how and why we accept professional invitations is an important consideration for the thriving musician. Carefully choosing professional invitations can become a vital and sometimes lucrative step in developing a career. Also consider that over time we may change what we want to do, that we often reach our professional goals, and that new vistas await us. You may find that what you did five years ago is no longer what you want to do today.

As you work with your business model, timeline, and your professional engagements and activities, be sure to develop your own sense of when "enough is enough." Give each task its time but no more; don't fuss. Avoid perfectionism because it will drag you down like quicksand. Musician and writer Diane Engle artfully draws our attention to a different notion of perfection in her tender poem "Autumn Apples."

> Take notice of the bruise, the artist said,
> For that's what I did best. Look closely. See,
> This blemish interrupts the field of red:
> I saw it right and showed it true. A tree
> That drops a perfect apple can't be real,
> Nor is the circle strictly round. Of course,
> This should not matter; little that we feel
> or love is without defect. Nothing's worse
> than picture-perfect people, flawless faces,
> angels fallen from their paradise
> to be transformed by falsehood that erases
> one line here, one there, to please the eyes.
> Still, I will have perfection when I'm through:
> The art, the art itself, seen right, shown true.[4]

Sometimes returning to your inner processes (listed in Chapter 5) can be useful in sustaining your energy and drive forward, bringing fresh inspiration, or simply quieting things, noticing what new synchronistic information is coming forward that may sculpt the development of your career. In creating your plan of action, remember that it is an ongoing process of "continuing education." Ask for help from others, find a mentor, network like crazy, attend conferences, conventions, and workshops; learn how to develop sponsorships, create consortia, consider a partnership, hire your own concert manager. When you need services, consider a professional "trade" with someone, create a critical mass of activity, invest in yourself (time and money), and be alert to serendipitous and synchronistic encounters. Farm every opportunity, read and study what you need to know. Develop other areas of intelligence that may be outside your greatest strengths. Enjoy the whole brain. Seek expert advice. In my own career, for example, I have hired professionals such as: consultants, publicists, photographers, public-relations people, accountants, attorneys, travel agents, and so on. When time has been of the essence, I have hired students, housekeepers, childcare providers, friends, and family to assist me. I have enrolled in grant-writing workshops, management seminars, career-planning workshops, business courses, artist retreats, master classes, and any number of assorted continuing-education opportunities. I regularly ask friends and colleagues for advice and I happily exchange what I have learned. It is a pleasure to give support to others as they pursue their dreams and goals. I encourage you to do the same. We are all members of the same arts community with an abundance of information and resources. Through networking and collaboration we thrive. When we are clear about our intentions and understand the concept of artistic service, all manner of support is available. In John Anster's rather free translation of Johann Wolfgang von Goethe's *Faust* from 1835, he writes: "What you can do, or dream you can, begin it, Boldness has genius, power, and magic in it."

One artist who beautifully exemplifies the work of a flourishing professional is violinist/violist Laura Klugherz. As a music entrepreneur and professor at Colgate University, she is in constant demand. Her most stunning work, however, has been with a number of underserved communities in Chile. In 1998, she was a guest violinist sponsored by the Fundación Andes and the Chilean Ministry of Culture in Concepción. As part of her outreach, she visited the remote mining community of Curanilahuc at the request of the music director, Américo Giusti, to help support a budding youth orchestra program. Later, as part of the National Federation of Youth Orchestras, this initiative was also the project of the Chilean first lady, Lucia Durán de la Fuente (2000–06), and Américo Giusti. Laura continued to assist this organization by working with youth from many rural orchestras in subsequent visits sponsored by the Ministry of Culture. Her services included youth master classes, professional retreats for orchestra directors, and clinics for string teachers. Laura's international career has thrived because in addition to being a fine performer and educator, her work as an artist is also about service to humanity and, most significantly, to underserved communities.

MENTORS FOR YOUR VISION–PLAN

Whatever vision–plan you craft and put into action, it can be particularly useful to have a mentor from time to time. No one builds a thriving career without help from others. Ideally, a mentor is a guide, a counselor, a wise mirror, and someone without a personal agenda for your unfolding destiny. These are primarily people who are on the same creative path but ideally much further ahead. They have triumphed over insurmountable odds, have endured the vagaries of life, and are truly thriving. They also have a particular joy in sharing what they know and have much wisdom to offer.

In the beginning stages of the planning process, a mentor can be your best asset. A skilled mentor can also help you avoid reinventing the wheel. In determining who might be a skilled mentor, consider the following criteria.

 EXAMPLE 6.4

QUALITIES OF AN IDEAL MENTOR

- Depth of wisdom
- Similar goals and artistic path
- Observable thriving
- No personal agenda for their clients
- Poised, relaxed, fully engaged in the present
- Using whole brain
- Good sense of humor
- Depth of compassion

A gifted mentor can serve as a valuable witness to your process, often validating your work, providing inspiration and encouragement when setbacks inevitably occur, and offering impartial feedback to the strategies you choose.

OTHER MUSIC ENTREPRENEURS: THE STUDENT AND THE RETIREE

In this book I have targeted the conversation mostly to midcareer professionals. Before we move onto the next chapter and those nuts-and-bolts topics such as developing your business model, creating realistic timelines, crafting your media materials, and choosing your professional advisers, I want to mention two other types of music entrepreneurs: the college or university student who is engaged in professional training, and the over-sixty entrepreneur who is in the period of life that author and psychologist Ken Dychtwald and contributing author Daniel J. Kadlec identify as "middlescence." Both these distinctive music entrepreneurs have particular challenges and gifts to offer the music industry.

Upon the completion of their professional training, students will be leaving the academic village for what Bensen referred to as the "sordid market place." As they launch their professional careers they will find that living as an entrepreneur can help them to thrive as they respond to changing economic conditions, shifts in the market place, and their own evolving career goals. These students are the future of the music industry and so their training is of paramount importance. Although there is national attention on new entrepreneurial initiatives, most colleges and universities find it difficult to add an entrepreneurship curriculum to their music degree programs, in the face of shrinking budgets and diminished resources. There are, however, a number of innovative strategies that can be included in the current music curricula at little or no cost. These are strategies that can help to prepare our music graduates for their careers and the various jobs they may pursue within those careers.

Three curricular cells can be inserted into most any music degree program without additional costs. They are as follows:

- Entrepreneurial advising: Working with students to address the vision–plan paradigm as early as the sophomore year. Begin referencing all academic and professional advising from this paradigm. Assign appropriate reading such as Richard Bolles's book *What Color Is Your Parachute?* or other targeted sources. Make a two- to three-year plan with specific entrepreneurial benchmarks, such as internships, that reflect career goals, plans for graduate school, or setting into place the networking process in preparation for a job search.
- Experiential learning: Providing students with hands-on experience in the "real world." Internships are great for this. They can be paid or unpaid but the key is to choose an internship that is directly on the career path of the student. An internship can also be the foundation for the research included in a senior thesis. Additionally, the world of volunteerism is a rich experiential resource. When students volunteer, they often make important professional contacts and they have the personal rewards that come with sharing their talents and helping others. Experiential learning can combine those two vital career components: networking and collaboration.
- Entrepreneurial instruction: Here students build their skill set through direct instruction. This can come in the form of workshops offered by visiting guest artists to campus, residencies on and off campus, networking with established professionals in the field, and even career development or grant-writing classes.

Much more can be said about the growing field of music entrepreneurship training. The above curricular strategies can be a start, however, in laying the groundwork for

lifelong learning and the development of music entrepreneurs, helping our graduates respond to undetermined future markets. For those of us who also serve as educators, it is critical to the health of our profession to include these experiences in our
teaching. The world of entrepreneurship requires each of us to expand our belief
system about the music profession. We want to impart this experience and knowledge to our students, the future of our profession. Although the complexities of the
future can at times be overwhelming, I believe it is far more interesting and prefer-
able to embrace this uncertainty than rigidly maintaining some historic status quo.
Let's do away with "We've always done it that way."

From his extensive work as a research psychologist and gerontologist, Ken Dychtwald
offers a radical view for retired entrepreneurs. In his groundbreaking book *With
Purpose: Going from Success to Significance in Work and Life*, Dychtwald suggests that
we are entering a revolution in terms of how we see the aging process. From roughly
age sixty and beyond, adults have acquired often decades of professional experience.
Because of increased longevity and prosperity, they often have the time and resources
to offer wisdom and mentorship to their families, communities, country, and the
world. In retirement, whether employed or not, this is the time when artists can bring
the full measure of their experience and knowledge to others, moving from success to
significance in their work. This notion of service is central to those musicians who are
thriving.

The idea of middlescence becomes a vital topic for midcareer professionals to
consider as they approach the traditionally held notion of retirement. No longer
a time to conclude on career dreams and activities, retirement can hold a golden
opportunity to reconnect to the world of service that lies outside the boundaries of
income production, career expansion, and employment concerns. With new political discussions in the United States emerging around social security and Medicare
reform, it may also be vitally important for retirees to continue some kind of income
production well into their elder years. With the aging of the "baby boomers," and
increased longevity, there may even be a new wave of political activism on behalf of
the elderly.

Research scientist and writer Elkhonon Goldberg offers a timely view of elder
wisdom, focusing on the gains of aging rather than cognitive losses. He includes
research from the field of neuroscience as well as case studies of real people, both
ordinary and famous, as they age. In his book *The Wisdom Paradox: How Your
Mind Can Grow Stronger as Your Brain Grows Older*,[5] he directs us to consider the
following ideas. Even though certain mental functions can decline through the
aging process, what continues to grow is the adult capacity to grasp the "big picture." Goldberg reminds us that the field of neuroscience has shown that the brain
can remain plastic, with continuing nerve cell regeneration into old age. His book

provides an important resource for ways to enhance brain function and cognitive fitness, and illuminates our understanding of the wisdom that can come from the aging process.

For most vitally engaged musicians, retirement can hold some measure of financial security and so those experiences of volunteerism and giving back to our communities can flower during those elder years. What better way to change and enrich our world than by giving freely of our talents and wisdom? As Dychtwald suggests: "You don't have to give away millions of dollars or devote every minute of your life to a grand cause. You just have to find your spot and be grateful for the opportunity to help in a way that brings you joy. There is a place and a calling for people who just want to lend a hand and spill the good vibes forward."

To those of you either entering or firmly planted in middlescence, I invite you to join the millions of retired volunteers as well as active music entrepreneurs who are changing the world. Be part of the ripple effect of this work.

In closing this chapter's discussion of the many considerations and key principles that go into making a vibrant plan of action, one final topic remains before we tackle the next chapter's discussion regarding the nuts and bolts of how to build that plan. The topic of prospering in the music industry is central to the thesis of this book. Conventional wisdom has held that having a career in the arts is next to impossible and even with a job, it is certainly not lucrative. Those who are thriving in the music industry, however, know this may be conventional thinking but it is far from accurate. Fortunately in 2011, a comprehensive national study was done that gathered data about the lives and careers of arts graduates. This research study included responses from 13,851 alumni from 154 different arts programs, including the following under graduate arts majors: dance, design, fine and studio arts, music performance, creative writing, media arts, film, architecture, and theater. This comprehensive survey was done by the Strategic National Arts Alumni Project (SNAAP) that is based at the Indiana University Center for Postsecondary Research at the School of Education. Dan Berrett, writing for *Inside Higher Ed*, an online resource for news, opinion, and jobs in higher education, reviewed this survey in his article "The Myth of the Starving Artist."[6] According to the project director, George Kuh, professor emeritus at Indiana, "This survey constitutes the largest dataset gathered about the lives and careers of arts graduates." Steven J. Tepper, associate director of the Curb Center for Art, Enterprise, and Public Policy, assistant professor in the department of sociology at Vanderbuilt University, and senior scholar for SNAAP, noted that the project results indicated that arts graduates were putting together diverse career options and employment along with strong indications of personal satisfaction. The survey also reflected that thriving artists tend to be highly entrepreneurial. Bill Barrett, executive director of the Association of Independent Colleges of Art and Design, said he was impressed by how many alumni had started their own businesses, "especially since we're always told that our nation depends on developing more creative, innovative entrepreneurs." Barrett added, "SNAAP demonstrates that arts alumni enjoy roughly the same levels of employment, and satisfaction with their education and their careers, as other college graduates."

Adding to this body of research, the National Endowment for the Arts, in June 2011, published the findings of its recent research project "Artist Employment Projections Through 2018." Their findings echo the work of SNAPP. "From 2008 to 2018, the U.S. labor force is expected to increase by 10%, or 15.3 million people. The professional-and-related occupations category, which includes artists, is projected to increase by nearly 17%, roughly seven percentage points higher than the projected growth rate for the U.S. labor force. At 11%, the projected growth rate for artists is similar to the rate projected for overall labor force growth (10%)."[7]

In realizing that you can bring to fruition your artistic visions and that you can create a vital musical career, you can dispel long-held caveats that have no truth in the market place. Instead, look to your own artistic vision and the concrete plan you are launching. This is your new musician's road map. Surround yourself with like-minded people, those artists who are thriving. Pay attention to how successful artists instigate and sustain their particular careers. Foster strong and inspiring connections with those individuals and organizations that need your talents. Build dynamic, innovative, and *lasting* consortia. Network and collaborate with enthusiasm and integrity. Cultivate your own ongoing continuing education. Bring joy to others through your work.

This chapter has presented key concepts concerning income production, grant writing, networking, consortia building, continuing education, collaboration models, and those principles that serve to build a strategic career plan of action. Our next topic targets the practicalities of building your plan, including the development of an effective business model.

7

YOUR PLAN: TAKING CARE OF BUSINESS

THIS GREAT SONG from the rock 'n' roll era of the 1970s says it all. It's what we do as entrepreneurs: take care of business. In earlier chapters I discussed how to develop an artistic vision, how to work with the imaginative and regenerative neuroplastic brain, and what important principles support a vibrant and innovative plan of action—your new musician's road map. This chapter will guide you in putting your own career plan into action. It's how *you* take care of business!

Though the topics of this chapter may be the ones that are least explored in the professional training of musicians, if you already are conversant with business models, strategic timelines, the Internal Revenue Service tax code, performance contracts, liability issues, media materials, social networks, and the like, then please feel free to proceed immediately to the next chapter, on higher education.

When we put our strategic plan into place, derived from our career vision, there is a host of components that are critical to success. While markets change and the lifelong journey of an artist can hold many creative visions, there are, nonetheless, a number of fixed elements that are essential to any successful career strategy.

Any career planning must begin with an effective and detailed business model, also referred to as a "business plan." In fact, a marketing campaign, an online identity, and the cadre of professional advisers one uses are all referenced from the business model. You have to know where you are going in order to know what you will need. Whether you are looking to create your own independent enterprise, climbing the ladder of the music industry, working in the nonprofit sector, or even thriving in the field of education, all roads lead to first creating your business model. This template allows you to think about your goals in a systematic way. It makes your planning *real*. There it is in black and white: who you are, your vision, your goods and services, your marketing strategies, the reality of your finances, a precise and doable timeline, and your advisory team of professionals. With a well-honed business model or plan, you will have the road map you need to achieve your goals. It's a map that is grounded in reality.

While I am offering a typical format for the business model, keep in mind that no two strategies will be the same. Every musician is different and so the particulars of each plan will be carefully tailored to the needs of the individual. Fortunately in today's global market place there is an abundance of readily available business information. Online is a great place to start and for most musicians, the Small Business Administration is the first stop (http://www.sba.gov). This government agency provides help to entrepreneurs in launching and sustaining their businesses. In partnership with the SBA, the nonprofit Service Corps of Retired Executives (SCORE) also offers assistance to small businesses and entrepreneurs by providing business counseling services at no charge. With some 13,000 volunteers nationwide, they offer the knowledge and experience to help any individual or enterprise with the mentoring and education they need. Their online site (http://www.score.org/about-score) is resplendent with information!

Most artists have heard about the notion of a business model or plan and have some general idea about why and how it is useful. A business model makes your musician's road map real. It validates your direction and demonstrates how you plan to reach your goals, and it can provide a reality check on the financial piece of your work. You will also need a professional business plan if you seek funding from a financial institution or the private investor. For the music entrepreneur, that business plan can serve as a map on a daily, monthly, and yearly basis. The irony, however, is that once you design this, be prepared to adapt it to your journey. Remember, you may build the road as you go.

Years ago, when I launched my website and decided to expand my consulting work, I had the benefit of sage advice from a former vice-president at Oracle. He decided at midcareer to take a daring move and retire from Oracle early—his chance to pursue new paths. With a passion for classical music, and great wisdom about the market place, he offered to help me reach my goals. We had many conversations about what I hoped to offer in my consulting, the kinds of clients I enjoyed helping, and the support I hoped to provide to my fellow musicians. The real challenge came, however, when he gave me the task of developing my new business model. There would be no website conversations or marketing plans until I was able to do that. It was, to say the least, a wake-up call. And in fact, it took me many months to somehow make sense of all the seemingly disparate things that fell under the rubric of "my professionals activities."

What I discovered from this assignment is that the nature of my work *is* diverse. I am not a carbon copy of any other music professional. Of course I share many activities in common with others but the kaleidoscope of my professional interests is what makes me who I am. It is central to my own artistic journey. I discovered that my distinct array of talents, skills, and experience would determine how I developed my business model. This would in turn be reflected in my website, marketing plan, and those clients that I wanted to assist. Through developing that detailed business plan, I also realized that I am not for everyone. I have a particular clientele that will benefit from the work I offer.

That business plan took me several months to write. Again, I found myself wrestling with the details, especially the unknown components that would have to unfold serendipitously. I learned that even though I was crafting a specific business model, paradoxically I also had to have a joyful willingness to scrap it if necessary! It was my business adviser who taught me about navigating these rocky shoals.

For every business model or plan, there are a number of fixed components that are essential. As you build your own model, you will need to consider how they reflect your work. The following are essential for all business models.

MISSION STATEMENT

Most business plans begin with a mission statement. For individuals, this can also be an artist statement. You will need to first describe who you are and what you are offering. What is your purpose in the market place? Presumably, you have done this personal work through the process of crafting your artistic vision—knowing what you want (the process described in Chapter 5). Whether you are an individual artist or a small business enterprise, this mission statement will be essential, much in the same way as it functions in effective grant writing. Not only does your reader learn about you, but you also benefit by being able to describe your identity in a concise narrative. This mission statement also serves as the foundation for building your marketing strategy as well as all your professional materials. I favor a 100-word mission or artist statement. If you are able to effectively write about what you do in this condensed format, then most likely you have a keen grasp of your mission. For the reader, brevity is essential.

Should you decide to expand your mission statement, keep it to no more than one page. Be mindful that the work you do up front on this narrative will be essential to all the other components of your business model. Moreover, it will be required if you are seeking funding from a financial institution or a granting agency. If you are stumped about how to write your statement, you can visit any number of online sites that present superb examples of real-life mission statements. Two excellent examples can be found on the following sites: the Gallo Center for the Arts (Modesto, California) and jazz composer and guitarist Nick Grondin. These beautifully honed mission statements give the reader a clear and concise view of their market, their particular focus in the music industry, and what they hope to accomplish. I invite you to visit these diverse narratives at:

http://www.galloarts.org/AboutUs/Mission.aspx
http://www.nickgrondin.com/artist-statement/

LEGAL IDENTITY

You will also need to describe your legal identity. Are you operating as a nonprofit, a limited liability company (LLC), an independent contractor, or as an employee of another business entity? Who you are legally will affect many of your financial decisions. In the grant-writing section of Chapter 6, for instance, I reviewed how your legal identity determines what kind of grant funding you can pursue. Should you seek support from a financial institution, you will be required to identify how your business functions legally. My personal recommendation, regardless of how you choose to operate as a business entity, is to have some kind of firewall in place in case of litigation. For many of us, a simple and inexpensive solution can be to form an LLC. Some entrepreneurs also include a nonprofit arm to their work. This is particularly useful if you are looking to acquire support from foundations and government agencies. Either way, legal documents have to be registered and will be part of your business model. An attorney and certified public accountant (CPA) can give you important guidance as you determine your legal persona.

GOODS AND SERVICES

For your business model or plan you will need to outline in great detail what goods and services you provide. The "goods" you provide are tangible products that you offer for sale. For example, you might sell your commercial CDs or DVDs, publications, arrangements, compositions, teaching materials, residency guides, instruments and parts, and so on. The "services" you provide, alternatively, usually fall under the rubric of helping with a need in the market place and would include such activities as: performances, teaching, residencies, consulting, and the like. Your services essentially offer some kind of helpful action and do not constitute work that makes something tangible. Your credible business plan will articulate the difference between the goods and services you offer. Furthermore, any product you make or service you provide should have a corresponding sample. This gives your reader an immediate grasp of your work. These samples might include such things as recordings, concert programs, residency guides, teaching materials, instruments and equipment, or publications. These will go into your detailed business plan. It gives concrete evidence of what you do. Be sure to also include your future projections. Are there new products and services that you would like to offer? If so, in what ways? What are your long-term plans regarding your current production of goods and services? How is it sustainable? What's the timeline?

Regardless of your career path, ultimately your goods and services are based upon one defining benchmark: what you offer is of the highest quality and your goods and services are unique in the market place. Not even the cleverest marketing campaign can make up for mediocrity, with perhaps the exception being in the television or film industry. Before you begin developing your business model, make sure you are prepared to offer something of extraordinary quality and value that has little duplication in the market place. While you may find that there are other professionals involved in your sphere of the music industry, you want to make sure that what *you* offer is distinctive, original, innovative, and answers to a clear need in the market place.

As I discussed in earlier chapters, most music entrepreneurs develop streams of income. These are the avenues of production for your goods and services. You will need to describe in detail these sources of revenue. What is it that you do or make, and how do you profit from it? Include current samples of what you offer and financial statements to back it up. Your yearly tax return can serve as credible evidence of this. Financial institutions usually require three years of income tax history. Be sure to include your future projections. Here you can demonstrate how each of these streams of income will serve you and say whether or not you plan to pursue these activities in the future. Be sure to describe how these sources of income are profitable and *sustainable*.

FINANCIAL PLAN

Speaking of income, you will need to produce a financial statement that itemizes your current revenue (after taxes) as well as overhead costs. What you are seeking is that magic number that reflects your net profit (revenue minus overhead = net profit). Those overhead expenses are tricky to track because small expenditures can be easily overlooked. Everything is important to document and that can mean including such items as: office supplies, postage, consultants, media materials, continuing education, travel, per diem, professional membership dues, books, website costs, professional activities, job searches, uniforms (concert gear, too), instrument purchases and repairs, equipment, and so on. If you have a penchant for spreadsheets and pie charts, it can be very useful to those who read your business plan to include a visual description of your financial circumstances. Remember to also include a three-year financial history of your enterprise as well as a three- to five-year projection of what you expect to develop. Again, your annual IRS tax return should have much of your past information. How do you plan to sustain your business? Give concrete evidence as to why you make your future projections. Are you basing your projections on evidence from the past? Do you have future contracts and commitments in hand? Is there reasonable expectation for advancement in your career? Are you currently engaged in income-producing work outside your career that is essentially funding the development of your career (the Charles Ives model)? Documentation is needed on all fronts! If you have an aversion to number crunching and other such "dark arts," you might want to consider some continuing education in the area of accounting or seek targeted help from your accountant.

Additionally, I would highly recommend that you assess your net worth. Add up the value of all your assets and subtract the liabilities you have. That will be your net worth. For example, if you have stocks and bonds worth $50,000 and a retirement account worth $100,000, but you owe $40,000 on your home, $5000 on your line of credit, and $10,000 on your car, then your net worth is $95,000. If you have equity in your home, then that is factored into your net worth as well. This is a much larger view of your financial picture, particularly when you want to reduce debt and increase savings. There it is in black and white. Joe Dominquez and Vicki Robin, in *Your Money or Your Life*, offer excellent strategies for increasing your net worth as well as doable exercises to help reduce debt. I highly recommend this publication for ongoing financial planning. If you are fortunate to have collateral resources such as a home, savings, retirement investments, or even an inheritance, you can parlay these assets into additional business support.

MARKETING

As you craft your business model you will be faced with a number of issues around marketing. Quite simply, business is about marketing! Whether it is online, in person, on the phone, in print, or the offhanded tweet, it's 24:7 for marketing. Every encounter and every communication you make is potentially a marketing opportunity. Without an effective marketing strategy, your talents and skills remain hidden. Certainly you have little chance of thriving.

A dynamic marketing plan is driven by what you offer in the way of goods and services, your fee for those services, what markets you wish to connect with (your promotional plan), whom you are helping with your products and services, and how much money you have available to spend on marketing tools. Lastly, you need to explain why someone should care about your work! For those music entrepreneurs new to the world of marketing, I have put together a Marketing Starter Kit. It's what is minimally required to move your enterprise forward, giving evidence in your business plan that you do indeed have a marketing strategy. This list also provides you with what you need to focus on first. There is no point in jumping into your networking campaign without these essential items.

 EXAMPLE 7.1

MARKETING STARTER KIT

1. Online presence (your professional website).
2. Hardcopy materials: stationery, business cards, rack cards, brochures, poster templates, résumé.
3. Photos.
4. Feature stories for media outlets (at least one 500-word and 1500-word narrative).
5. Product samples for marketing (this can include items such as: commercial recordings, writing samples, educational materials, residency guides, etc.).
6. Professional contracts.
7. References (review of your work from other respected professionals or media outlets).

Having these materials in place gives credence to your professionalism. These components can also be attached to your business plan in the form of an appendix. From here you will need to identify where you intend to offer your goods and services and what advertising and publicity campaign you intend to launch. It is important to remember that all your materials (website, business cards, stationery, media pieces, posters, etc.) must be of the highest quality and that they tell your potential clients about the nature and substance of your work. How are you serving their needs? What solutions are you offering to their challenges? Remember, you get only one "first impression." That initial contact with your clientele is crucial. Put your best foot forward, whether it is on the phone, online, or in hard copy. Your business model should reflect your high-caliber marketing tools and the dynamic work you intend to launch.

Early in my professional life I encountered Terry Mandel, a gifted marketing professional who essentially helped to launch my career. Because Terry is a natural-born teacher, I easily became her willing student. Terry's wisdom regarding marketing, living in authenticity, and producing high-quality work is well documented. She provided me with superb promotional materials, a compelling press kit, and was the publicist for my New York debut. Terry showed me how important it was that all my materials reflect the highest standards. She also coached me on how to be persistent, especially on the phone. For the myriad of booking conferences I attended early in my career, she prepared me on how to "work the crowd," in the best sense of the word. No detail was ever too small and when discouragement set in, she reminded me to keep my sights set on my artistic vision. Things would work out if I applied myself to my art and to the heart of my marketing.

For this book, I asked Terry to share a brief narrative on marketing that would be useful to a diverse array of professional musicians looking to strengthen their entrepreneurial skills, change direction in their careers, or simply launch new and innovative initiatives. She graciously offered this sage advice.

I've had the privilege of working with many extraordinary artists in my thirty-plus years as a marketing and management consultant and mentor. Despite the unique approach each brings to her/his artistic expression, nearly all share an aversion to self-promotion that limits the likelihood of their success.

When I ask artists to share their dreams with me, they naturally focus on the culmination of many years of hard work—triumphant recitals in desirable venues, glowing reviews in prestigious publications, successful recording projects, attractive commissions, enviable collaborations, wide recognition. When I ask what they imagine it will take to bring these about, they often point to signing with a well-connected agent who can make it all "happen." It's when I ask what they think it will take to get on that agent's radar or roster, that anxiety begins to creep in. Many will ask, "Well, isn't that your job?" I can help artists transform their attitudes about marketing from something awful they "have to do," to a strategic, and authentic, form of expression that supports their dreams coming true. I can help artists learn that the career they long for is built not just through becoming excellent at their craft but skillful in shaping their professional lives. I can help artists get over the ubiquitous belief that they don't have the right kind of personality to be successful marketers, as if only extroverts, shameless self-promoters, or those "lucky enough" to find the "right agent" get ahead. What I can't do—however brilliant the artist or dedicated and skillful I am (or other professionals are)—is give anyone the career of their dreams. It's very clear that those who succeed are able to expand their sense of their "art" to include every aspect of sharing their unique gifts with audiences, from developing marketing and promotional strategies, materials, and platforms, to choosing and directing professionals who help them grow as they do their bit to help bring the artist's dreams to fruition, as well as offering heartfelt performances that touch something deep in their listeners. Because marketing is often used in obnoxious ways, many people have concluded that marketing is obnoxious. This is a career-threatening mistake that artists are particularly prone to making. Marketing is a simply a tool, one perfectly designed to share the beauty of what you do—that is, who you are—with the very people likely to be touched by that.

I had fun working with Terry and what started out as a professional relationship quickly blossomed in to a deep friendship. I still learn from Terry and share her wisdom with my students. Most of all, Terry taught me an important truth and one that I hope you will take to heart: *You can never pay anyone enough to care about your career more than you do.*

MANAGEMENT TEAM

With all effective business plans, you will need to also describe your management team. Whether you are an independent contractor, the owner of a small enterprise, or an employee of a larger business, you will need a team of advisers to assist you with all manner of ongoing tasks. They will be crucial to your career planning and success. In your business plan you will present their credentials and describe how they are contributing to the successful operation of your business. These professionals can include, but are not limited to: an attorney, certified public accountant, financial planner, manager or agent, publicist, graphic designer, copyeditor, collaborative artists, as well as various consultants, investors, and so on. What is important to note in your business model is that you *have* an advisory staff in place. In other words, you are not simply going it alone, hoping that whatever business acumen you have will suffice. If we are attending to the high quality of our professional offerings, there is little time available to acquire the necessary expertise in all the areas we will need in order to develop our prosperous careers. Even with a multiskilled artist such as Lauren Pelon, you will still find in the background an attorney, CPA, and financial planner. It is the wise entrepreneur who knows when and whom to ask for help.

Of the aforementioned professionals, three are absolutely required. Without an attorney, a CPA, and a financial planner you can encounter real (and costly) problems in the music profession. For those professionals who will read your business plan, it is a must to have these three experts represented. This gives you credibility outside your artistic accomplishments. No one in the business world today operates successfully without them!

Before you say, "but I can't afford these costly professionals," consider the alternative. Are you prepared to do your own taxes, being fully aware of the morphing tax code for limited liability companies (LLCs), nonprofit organizations, or simply the Schedule C on the standard return? Before I landed my current CPA some twenty years ago, I found myself audited twice by the IRS. Like most musicians, I have a rather atypical tax return. At the time of the audits, I was a college professor with a separate business that operated under the Schedule C. I survived both audits because I kept meticulous records. Nevertheless, it was stressful and time-consuming. What I discovered once I acquired a CPA is that I had a tax professional guiding my business. She was up to date on tax law, the often-changing landscape of deductions, she provided me with valuable tools in record-keeping, and was prepared to stand with me should I be audited. She provided me with financial advice and in the long run I saved time and money having her on my "staff."

I eventually graduated to an LLC for liability purposes (my legal firewall) and at the time of this writing, I still keep my own books. My CPA prepares my tax return but more importantly she frequently offers money-saving tips, new tax breaks, and ways of making my dollars stretch further. In fact, the first year I went with her, she insisted on filing an amended return for the previous year, garnering me additional refund dollars.

The other essential member of your professional team is an attorney. Yes, attorneys are costly. But in the United States we live in a litigious society. To turn a blind eye to this fact is to court trouble. In my opinion, you will save much in the way of money and heartache if you bring an attorney on board early in your career planning. They can alert you to important legal issues to consider and produce high-quality damage-proof contracts.

As a professional musician, you can operate as an LLC or as a nonprofit. Some choose to do both. Most of us will opt for the LLC route because it is simpler to launch and it also provides a firewall to anyone who wishes to pursue litigation. For up-to-date legal advice regarding your interest in forming either an LLC or your own nonprofit arts organization, see a qualified attorney who has experience and interest in the arts. These professionals are important specialists in the field. Don't necessarily rely on your best friend's divorce attorney or your parent's estate attorney. They may have little information about entertainment law.

Once you venture out as an entrepreneur, providing a myriad of services to individuals and communities, you will need various contracts. Some will be for performances, others for workshops, clinics, public-school residencies, and the like. You may also be responding to employment contracts, collective bargaining, and independent-contractor agreements. What you want to avoid is costly litigation. For example, if you have a misunderstanding with a presenter and you don't receive what was agreed, you could spend thousands of dollars to receive what is rightfully yours. A lawsuit of this nature can often include interstate litigation and sometimes even international considerations. You want to avoid this from happening. This also holds true for an employment contract with a single employer. Before you accept a job, have the contract reviewed by an attorney. You will be glad you did!

Most people you encounter in the performing arts are honest. They are working hard to bring live music and corresponding educational events to their communities. Difficulties that arise often stem from poor or insufficient communication. When things are in writing via a contract, everyone can see what has been agreed and so misunderstandings are brought to a minimum. And the more details you include, the better. Leaving your presenter, a nonprofit, a consortium, sponsors, or an employer with a positive experience can insure repeat business. Don't assume that everyone understands what it is that you do, and what it is that you need to do it!

Written agreements are also essential when you choose to volunteer your time. Whether they are paid or not, exquisite communication is needed for artists as they move into the professional world. For the most casual of activities even a simple letter of intent or agreement will suffice. The key is to avoid misunderstandings in communication. Keeping a detailed paper trail of all your communications is essential. Email is a great tool for this record-keeping, confirming verbal agreements and providing an account of those details that may fall outside the realm of a formal contract.

There are other considerations as well regarding those formal contracts. Although payment is a major part of a contract, there are a host of other conditions that require clear and detailed explanation. Over the course of many years, I have added a number of stipulations to my various contracts. Inevitably these add-ons were the result of something going wrong with a particular event. Keep in mind that they involve my work as a pianist, but there are equivalencies in other areas of the music profession. If you can imagine something going wrong, it's best to head that off in your contract. Here are just a few examples of what I added to my contracts.

- I require an adjustable bench. (Even though this seems obvious for a formal piano recital, I have actually encountered an office chair waiting for me on stage!)
- The hall must be heated to at least 68 degrees Fahrenheit. (When I arrived at one concert venue a couple of hours before my performance, the temperature was 55 degrees Fahrenheit! Although the presenter later turned on the heat, the hall remained well below 68 degrees, requiring me to perform in a heavy wool sweater as an accoutrement to my concert gown!)
- Lighting is always spelled out in my contracts. Each performer has a specific set of standards. For pianists, a double set of shadows on the black keys

can be disastrous. When I have used my car for transportation, I have often taken my own floor lamp, extension cord, extra bulbs and even my own adjustable piano bench.

- The stage must be clean, clear of all debris or materials from an earlier performance, and it must be level. (This seems obvious, but I have arrived before curtain to find all manner of stands, music, chairs, and lighting from other presentations. One performance space actually had a stage that was not level!)

- Filming and still photos have to be spelled out in every contract. (It is not unusual for someone in the audience to bring their recording equipment, especially for master classes and lectures. There are all types of legal violations when this occurs. Needless to say, the participants in a master class have not given permission for others to film them. Aside from that, you have to decide if you are okay with suddenly appearing on YouTube! Take special care not only with your work but be mindful of group settings where others may not wish to have their image photographed or their work recorded.)

- For transportation, housing, and per diem, I recommend that you negotiate with the presenter that they pay directly for these expenses. When the presenter buys your plane ticket, for example, that is not part of your taxable income. In the long run this can save you money.

These are just a few examples of contract points. There are countless other considerations, depending upon your individual needs. The contracts we negotiate bring to the fore all the crucial points for both employee and employer. When all is said and done, however, it is the attorney who sculpts the final agreements. Whether you are working from streams of income or for one business entity, with solid written arrangements in place, you have the best insurance available for successful, profitable, and dynamic partnerships, ones that may well include a long-term relationship with an employer!

The third essential member of your advisory team is the certified financial planner. This is a professional whose certification is awarded in the United States by the Certified Financial Planner Board of Standards, Inc. These financial advisers help individuals and businesses with such issues as insurance, retirement, investment, and estate planning. They also offer guidance concerning cash flow and risk management, education planning, and business oversight. Their input often intersects with that of the attorney and CPA. The resources they offer, however, are much broader and have to do with long-term financial considerations. A good planner will assist you with the financial issues of your business model. They can also provide outside scrutiny, not to mention long-term financial planning for your career. Costs for their services vary. Many operate on a percentage basis through retirement plans or investment programs.

As you work with your management team, other crucial considerations will emerge. Either with an LLC or a nonprofit, liability insurance will be important. For those professionals who work out of their home office, most home insurance policies will provide a business rider. If not, you can contact your national professional organizations for advice. The Music Teachers National Association, for example, offers a group liability policy to their membership. Avoid operating without this protection.

OTHER MEMBERS OF YOUR MANAGEMENT TEAM

Your attorney, CPA, and financial planner work for you on an ongoing basis and although they are in the background, they should have a thorough grasp of your work. Periodically, though, you may need other professionals as well. You may find that you require occasional help from a variety of specialists such as, but not limited to, marketing agents, publicists, web designers, copyeditors, or graphic artists. These specialists are useful for a specific job that requires a high level of expertise. My advice is that when you hire these people, learn from them. Consider it as an "in-service experience." Ask questions, be curious about how things are done; request a demonstration of those tasks you wish to take on yourself. Lauren Pelon, for example, became the master of many skills through this process.

There is much more to say about which specialists can best assist us. An artist's individual needs, however, will drive where and from whom they seek help. In addition to those professionals that can assist you, seek information from special publications that focus on one or two areas of need. For example, you may need help with your résumé, cover letters, business cards, websites, social networks and the Internet, using the phone, accessing sales conventions, and deciding whether to hire an agent or professional management. Marketing, too, is a vast universe. My advice is to educate yourself as to what the "gold standard" is for whatever you are looking to develop, keeping in mind that new information is continually available in the market place. The bibliography of this book has many suggestions but each artist must determine for himself or herself what it is that they need to know. The life of a music entrepreneur includes ongoing research! Moreover, consider connecting with someone in your field whom you clearly admire and who is thriving. Buying a few hours of their time could be one of your best investments. Find out how *they* managed to do well. That encounter might also fall under the earlier topic of networking: whom do they know who could help you, what resources would they recommend for you to investigate? You may also wish to consider a marketing consultant. Sometimes a skilled professional can move you forward quickly and teach you essential things for the successful development and promotion of your career.

TIMELINES

Returning to the topic of the business model there is one final component that you will need to articulate: your timelines. I consider both short-term and long-term templates. All strategies are ultimately grounded in *when* you plan to take a specific action. I prefer to start with two large-scale timelines, remembering that things can change as I begin my journey. I also recommend using a year-at-a-glance calendar. If you post it in your office, you are likely to see it everyday. It's a visual reminder of how you plan to stay on track.

The first timeline to address is the five-year template. This structure gives you a broad brush stroke of what you will need to put in place on a yearly basis. It can also articulate the culmination of what you wish to accomplish, based upon your artistic vision. For example, in five years you may want to have acquired national reviews for your work, published an important book, produced a commercial recording, achieved tenure in a job, reached a certain financial goal, secured your successful business track record. Your reference point is the artistic vision you have already carefully crafted. What is your perfect future five years from now? The answer to that question will drive your five-year timeline.

Following the five-year template is the one-year timeline. This grounds you in a full calendar year, the changing seasons, scheduling around holidays and vacations, the ebb and flow of the market place, and more specifically the focus for each month. You can fill in with weekly goals and even a kind of daily plan as well. For example, I reserve one hour a day for checking in on my planning process, assessing what needs to be done and in what sequence, what has been completed, and whether or not the schedule is working. Sometimes this hour becomes damage-control time. It's important to be flexible, especially if you get behind.

If you have difficulty identifying your objectives and the necessary tasks that must ensue, then most likely you are probably not clear about what it is you want to achieve. This could be an opportune moment to use the journaling process described in Chapter 4. This "idea book" can capture the creativity and clarity that falls outside the scrutiny of the conscious mind. I prefer to use pencil and paper because writing makes it real. In time, you can gain much information from this process. Rereading Chapter 5 can also be useful!

Although you will be articulating a specific set of long-term and short-term timelines for your business plan, life happens. Sometimes we achieve our goals ahead of schedule, at other times we can encounter setbacks and disappointments, and occasionally we simply change our direction based on new information. It's perfectly normal. The key here is to adapt. Remember, thriving entrepreneurs are ready for change. So even though you are designing specific timelines for your business model, they most likely will change once your journey is underway.

FINANCING YOUR PLAN

As musicians, we are all too familiar with the costs involved in entering our profession. Most of us have engaged in private study throughout childhood. Instruments we play cost money. Travel, continuing education, master classes, festivals, and the like are part and parcel of our professional investment. Supporting your business model is no different. It will require your time and money. There are, however, a number of ways of economizing.

I am a firm believer in the "professional trade." It's the old barter system. What can you offer to someone free of charge in exchange for the services you need? For example, I have seen clients and colleagues offer such things as a performance, a series of applied lessons, help with event planning, grant-writing advice, and copyediting in exchange for business support. Not only is this a win-win situation for both parties, it also serves to expand networking possibilities. Once again, consider what Gardner described in Chapter 6, those particular "intelligences" you might have. How can you assist others? This becomes your trade currency.

You can also look to friends and family who genuinely want to help you prosper. If you have specialists in your midst, ask for the support you need. I recommend, however, that you keep your request to something minimal and easily accomplished within a short time frame. Most people lead hectic lives. You want to avoid burning out your inner circle of supporters. For example, one of my colleagues has her father simply review all her grant applications. His long-standing career success with multimillion-dollar grant awards has proven to be a tremendous asset to her.

Also consider looking to your array of talents and skills. You may be able to provide your own graphic design, copyediting, media kit, promotional work, accounting, and the like. Think back to Lauren Pelon's professional story in Chapter 6. Because she is talented in so many areas, she rarely hires outside help. You might discover that you can do this as well.

In order to launch our enterprises, we sometimes need to seek outside financing. Most musicians are quite familiar with this process when they buy a musical instrument. This is where your carefully honed business plan becomes an important tool as you approach financial institutions. Although I caution artists about taking on the weight of large debt, a modest business loan can be particularly useful at the beginning of your journey. Look to your management staff for advice and feedback about your financing strategies. Consider what collateral you already have in place. Identify those financial institutions that have a track record of loaning to small businesses and individuals. You may also want to approach your own bank or credit union where you already have a financial track record.

As you begin the process of developing your business model, look to organizations such as SCORE and the Small Business Administration for support. You will find useful generic templates to build your business. I also recommend David Gumpert's book *How to Really Create a Successful Business Plan*. Now in its fourth edition, this pragmatic book offers helpful exercises, a sample business plan, and stories from well-known enterprises. Gumpert sympathizes with those who may be dreading the prospect of writing that professional business plan or model by offering specific help and encouragement. Richard Bolles also continues to be an excellent resource for those artists looking to start their own businesses. In *What Color is Your Parachute?* Bolles includes a separate chapter on starting your own business.

Your local college or university is a valuable source as well, offering continuing education in all types of business skills. Be mindful of your particular "intelligences," as well as those areas you most need to develop. Perhaps your business plan needs more detailed information in the financial area, or maybe a marketing professional is the right specialist to hire. Don't forget that your business plan launches your artistic vision. Whether you use it for outside support or rely on it for your own strategic planning, it is your road map. Consider the following checklist to get you started in your own planning.

BUSINESS PLAN CHECKLIST

Your business plan is a record of decisions that you must make about achieving a set of goals. Realize that much of your plan will be speculative. For example, you can't be certain what your true costs are until you have been in business for a while. You may have a targeted market in mind but you won't know for sure the most effective way to reach it and to create repeat business until you have tested your marketing plan. You will have a timeline in place for this plan but you may discover that things move more quickly or simply take more time. Be flexible. Your business plan will get you started but be prepared to rely on the feedback from actually doing your business. Sometimes we build the road as we go.

The following questions can help to individualize your business plan. Depending upon where you are on your vision–plan continuum, you may be brand new to this process or well underway with your business planning. Either way, these questions can send you in the right direction. For a more comprehensive worksheet, including a timeline template and details about identifying your competition, please download the Business Plan Worksheet.

 EXAMPLE 7.2

A. Mission or artist statement
1. Who are you in the market?
2. What goods or services do you provide?
3. What need in the market do you fulfill?
4. Why are you best qualified to fulfill this need?
5. Can you limit your narrative to 500 words?
6. Can you describe your business in one sentence? (This will allow you to speak concisely to potential clients.)

B. Legal identity
1. Are you a for-profit or nonprofit entity? (Perhaps both.)
2. Do you have liability insurance?
3. Do you have the necessary legal documents in place (i.e., contracts, tax identity, etc.)?
4. Do you have an attorney in place who is familiar with your work and who has oversight of your legal considerations and contracts?
5. Do you have a CPA for tax and financial advice?
6. Are you planning to seek support from financial institutions or venture capitalists and if so, do you have a professional financial statement in place?

C. Goods and services (your "product")
1. What is the product you offer? (Be clear about what you don't do!)
2. What is the cost to you to produce this product? (That would be your wholesale cost.)
3. What price will you offer your customers and is this a cost that the market will bear?
4. What do your customers consider "good value"?
5. What sort of profit margin can you expect?
6. What does your competition charge?
7. If you need it, do you have additional income sources available as you build your business?

D. Marketing
1. Where are you located?
2. Who are your potential customers?

3. Do you have a rough idea of how many people need your product?

4. Are you matching your product to the right customer?

5. What do these customers need and can you describe how you are the right person to help them?

6. Why should they go to you and not your competition?

7. How are you different from your competition?

8. How do you plan to get the message out to those customers about the product you offer in a cost-effective way?

9. Where do your clients and professional leaders do business? Where do they socialize or hang out?

10. What benefits and results do your clients receive from your product?

11. Do you have a plan to create repeat business from a growing clientele?

12. What will cause your clients to recommend your business to friends and colleagues?

13. Have you put together your Marketing Starter Kit?

E. Operations plan
   1. Timelines
      a. Do you have a five-year and a one-year timeline in place?
      b. What do you need right away to start your business?
      c. What do you need to *do* right away to move your business forward?
   2. Office setup
      a. Do you have the necessary equipment to operate your business? If not, how do you plan to acquire what is necessary?
      b. How do you operate onsite versus offsite?
      c. Is your legal identity in place?
      d. Do you have a business banking account?
      e. Do you have in place your tax preparation and record keeping?

F. Getting help
   1. What professionals do you need to assist you with your business? (You will need an attorney, CPA, and financial adviser. Additionally, you may need graphic designers, web specialists, marketing professionals, technicians, office staff, etc.)
   2. What consortia can you build to expand your work and create dynamic business partnerships?
   3. Do you have an ongoing networking plan to connect you with an ever-widening population of both clients and colleagues?
   4. Are there books and other resources, conferences or conventions, seminars or workshops that may offer you further guidance or help you to make connections?

The more detailed and articulate you are about the various business-model components presented in this chapter, the more efficient you will be, remembering that while your overall plan may be specific to your journey, it should be also flexible and open to serendipity. And sometimes you build the road as you go.

8

MUSIC JOBS IN HIGHER EDUCATION

ALTHOUGH THIS BOOK has eschewed any discussions about specific jobs in the music industry, one area deserves mention since it represents an important and overarching source of support in the music profession. In the United States, higher education offers extensive across-the-board support for the arts. In the music industry alone, according to the 2011 online report by the College Music Society, 42,895 professionals teach music in higher educational institutions throughout the country.[1] A book that explores career development in music would be incomplete without a special chapter on the world of higher education in the United States.

In many ways, higher education can be likened to the venerable model of arts patronage that the eighteenth-century court system provided. One of the best examples of this model is found in the life of Franz Joseph Haydn. He served as the resident court composer in the remote Austrian outpost of Esterháza, working for the Esterházy family for over thirty years. Moreover, through his court appointment he engaged in many of the same activities as today's music faculty. Like most academics, Haydn wore many hats: composer, teacher, arts administrator, host to visiting artists, and entrepreneur. And he was a mentor to other composers, including both Mozart and Beethoven.

With Prince Nikolaus Esterházy, Haydn was fortunate to find a supportive patron, but he was also extremely clever in how he developed his appointment. Haydn's humor is legendary; for example, in presenting the prince with works such as the Surprise Symphony or the Farewell Symphony, he was able to improve working conditions for his musicians as he further enhanced his own musical environment. And so, while faithfully serving the prince, Haydn, as a true entrepreneur, was able to develop his own gifts as a brilliant composer. His remarkable output is a reminder that musical careers are not necessarily made in just the most affluent urban centers, nor does any jay-oh-be necessarily constitute a career. We know Haydn as one of the great Classical composers and, incidentally, he worked as a court musician. His job in the court, however, was not his career. By the time he received invitations to London, he was a well-known and highly revered composer. If you are interested in launching your career through higher education, Haydn's biography is a must read. An excellent source is H. C. Robbins Landon's *Haydn: Chronicle and Works* series.

As Haydn found at his richly rewarding post at the court in Esterháza, so today's music professionals can find in higher education opportunities for performance, research, faculty development support, collaborative partnerships, stimulating students, and a steady income that often comes with a substantial benefit package. For some, it is a welcome job, often providing an important centerpiece to a diverse musical career.

Colleges and universities in many ways have formed the backbone of financial, creative, and educational resources for performing artists, scholars, concert presenters, and arts administrators. Each one of these professionals has a home in higher education. Depending upon the size of the institution, the variety and breadth of professional opportunities can be far reaching. The world of academia also contains a wealth of financial, research, collegial, and educational resources for musicians. In fact, a church-music post is the only other setting in the United States that comes close to this kind of job, and then only with those churches or synagogues that have substantial resources for a full-time director of music and with a corresponding operational budget.

The College Music Society and the National Association of Schools of Music are the main professional organizations for music professionals in higher education. For most institutions, they set the benchmarks and provide accreditation for a vast array of diverse degree programs. The challenge for many musicians is how to function within these programs that essentially require day-to-day commitments of academe along with real-world engagement as artists. Many academics labor under the "publish or perish" mandate. For musicians, that may also include performances, recordings, guest residencies, or concert tours. In a very real sense, musicians may find that in academia they choose to be in it but not of it. Their careers are firmly planted in the "sordid market place." So while trends shift in academia, while administrators come and go, and while funding has its ebb and flow, musicians can continue to thrive, knowing that their careers are simply the container for whatever jobs they choose, including a tenure-track appointment in higher education.

ENTERING THE WORLD OF HIGHER EDUCATION: THE PRICE OF ADMISSION

As with many professional appointments, there are countless hoops that one must jump through in order to join the institution. Higher education is no different.

Most musicians who want to be employed in higher education with a tenure-track appointment will need to complete their professional training through the doctorate level. Occasionally some musicians and scholars are brought into the institution through what is termed "equivalency." Usually, however, this is an artist or scholar who has obtained substantial credits at the international level.

There are a number of important considerations if a musician elects to go the route of acquiring a doctoral degree. Choosing the right program is essential. In today's market place, there are a growing number of doctoral programs that cater to the musician who is working full time. The EdCT program at Columbia University Teachers College is one such innovative program, offering online courses throughout the academic year and an intensive course of study during the summers. Boston University, as another model, offers a DMA in music education that requires periodic short residencies as a supplement to their online curriculum. The archaic model of several years of onsite residency is no longer the only option for graduate study. Many universities are now providing innovative and rigorous online programs requiring a blend of short-term on-campus residence along with web-based instruction.

If you are wondering about what time is right for engagement in a doctoral program, I would suggest that *now* can be the best time. By that I mean that any age can be the right time. With a shift in demographics vis-à-vis the baby-boomer generation, new models are appearing. I know of one music professional who began her doctoral studies at age sixty-two. I have a close friend who started her law school education at age fifty-three and went on to become a pro-tem judge. Is there an age limit to learning or self-actualization? I think not. And those who begin their doctoral studies later in life then have a wealth of professional experience to enhance both their studies and their job search. In the final analysis, however, each individual must weigh the personal cost of higher education with both intrinsic and professional rewards.

So from the start, a substantial investment of time and money is required before you have your admission ticket to academe. There are a number of ancillary posts for music professionals outside the teaching area that include such jobs as music librarian, media specialist, performing-arts series administrator, recording engineer, facilities director, and numerous staff and administrative support personnel. For the purposes of this narrative, however, I have chosen to focus on the teaching end of academia.

Once you land a position in higher education, a new process unfolds. If you enter as a tenure-track professor, then you begin the long ascent to what is most often permanent employment. Usually the tenure process takes six years, although if you come to academia with prior work that has academic currency, you can sometimes shorten the tenure process by a year or two. Few professionals are awarded tenure when they sign their initial contract. Beyond tenure the ascent continues, culminating with the rank of full professor. While much of the narrative in this chapter centers on the tenure process, the same principles and overarching requirements continue for the subsequent path to promotion.

For many music professionals, the evidence-based evaluation for tenure can be challenging at best. Most institutions of higher education use three assessment criteria for tenure awards and ensuing promotions: teaching, service to the institution, and professional activity. Of these three areas, professional activity for musicians can be the most difficult area to document in ways that administrators have traditionally valued. For instance, the adage "publish or perish" may not necessarily apply to a performing artist. For those music professionals, one might find career activities that include concert tours, commercial CDs, master classes, and the like. Research can be part of the performer's dossier but that research may have served to prepare a concert program or a commercial recording instead of appearing in print media.

Many performing artists find themselves tucked away in dusty archives searching for that special score that has not been published or recorded. Frequently you will find commercial recordings that have their genesis in academia. Passionate musicians looking to specialize in a certain genre or with a particular composer often feature those little-known composers whose works are unpublished or unrecorded. Some performing artists champion living composers, bringing to light contemporary voices.

Taking our performance credits into the tenure process requires careful strategy. To have tenure or promotion currency in the performing arts requires documentation and presentation in a language that nonmusicians will understand as well as your informed departmental colleagues.

For teaching as well as service to the institution, again, the issue is documentation in a language that is clear and underscores value—value to the institution as well as the larger professional world. Many of the courses that are offered in music departments fall under the category of "experiential learning." In short, that means students are able to derive meaning and information from a direct experience. They acquire this meaning through a process of "doing." As musicians, we all know the value of making music, both at a spiritual level and as an experience in the temporal world. Since colleges and universities require clear evidence of how goals, objectives, and competencies are met in the classroom, music professionals need to incorporate concrete assessment tools into their syllabi for those experiential courses. For this, the National Association of Schools of Music is a useful resource, offering concrete guidelines to the accreditation process.

How we document our temporal activities in music is of critical importance, particularly for those professionals outside the music profession. Much of the tenure process requires educating our colleagues across campus as to the rigors of music making, the enormous preparation that must be in place, and the types of effective assessment tools that are familiar to us. Being in the music profession can blind you to the fact that others in academia may not know about jury exams, capstone recitals, juried competitions, and adjudications. It is our responsibility as music professionals to document and describe fully what we do as rigorous professionals.

Service to the institution is the third area of assessment for tenure or promotion. This activity is somewhat easier to document. A candidate demonstrates the quality of personal commitment to the institution through the service component. In other words, you demonstrate as a faculty member that you are not singularly concerned with just your professional career or teaching load. You can provide evidence of care and engagement with the institution that is not mandated by contractual agreements. It can be, however, a bit of a slippery slope. I have known colleagues who became mired in too much activity in the area of service and consequently their teaching and professional commitments suffered. But if you keep in mind that your goal in the service assessment is to demonstrate your interest in serving the institution beyond professional concerns or teaching assignments, you will spend your time wisely. In no way, however, will the area of service make up for inadequate teaching or scarce professional activity. In providing evidence of your service to the institution, it's best to focus on a few points of engagement that are well defined, have specific time commitments, and are in the areas of your talents and skills. Some faculty prefer academic governance, others enjoy going on the road recruiting students, and many find important opportunities in bridging the institution to local communities. Choosing service activities that fit well with your skills and interests can also provide you with important and generative connections with your colleagues.

ACADEMIA: THE IDEAL

Why then higher education? Because in the right environment you can have artistic independence, excellent colleagues and friends, a national network of like-minded individuals, support for creativity, and best of all, wonderful and inspiring students.

The joy in my career has been to share music around the world as a performing artist in both live performances and commercial recordings and to nurture the next generation of musicians. I have been lucky to discover a good match for my skills and talents and the mission of the college where I work.

The success of any college or university is largely based on the hiring and retention of fine professionals. With the performing artist, it can be a challenge to hire and retain the right individual. A charismatic artist, however, can give a personal face to the college and often garner exceptional media coverage. Claude Frank at Yale University, János Starker and György Sebök at Indiana University, and Jascha Heifetz at the University of Southern California are just a few examples of luminary performing artists who have graced academia. And for those musicians who have more modest careers, there are countless opportunities to bring local and regional attention to institutions of higher education. Concerts, workshops, and festivals are all the kind of events that attract media attention—the kind that cannot be purchased by a college or university.

In higher education, a performing artist works in the professional world of concert performances and commercial recordings while simultaneously combining the necessary scholarly background and passion for teaching and mentoring of college students. This kind of musician also needs to be entrepreneurial in nature since much of the work for performing artists involves auditions, concert invitations, some artist self-management, promotional skills, creative programming, and event development (such as conferences, music festivals, guest-artist workshops, and so on).

A performing artist can be a partner with the college or university in the promotion, recruiting, and advertising of the institution and its mission. Often that can be as an ambassador to the local community and beyond. A performance review, a feature story, or concert previews are all media opportunities that are highly valued in higher education.

Typically, a resident artist carries an academic load but also must leave campus on a regular basis in order to fulfill their mission as a performer. This kind of musician also requires daily practice to maintain and develop skills, learn new programs, and literally stay in shape to perform at peak level. As with our colleagues in sports, there can be no last-minute training or preparation.

In all these pursuits, performing artists need to provide administrators, and ultimately a tenure or promotion review board, with concrete evidence of high-quality service, professional success, and teaching excellence.

In smaller departments, where few roles are duplicated, it is of paramount importance that faculty work in harmony and share in curricular responsibilities, recruiting, programming, committee work, and advising. Excellent departmental leadership is key in sharing the work load so that those who are pursing tenure are not overly burdened with those courses or responsibilities that senior faculty wish to avoid.

A job in higher education can also provide a number of excellent resources for performing artists and scholars. As an academic, you most often have access to a superb library, a state-of-the-art office, technology tools, fine instruments, capable students, collaborative professionals, and the pleasure of connecting with inspiring interdisciplinary colleagues across campus. When you have a small music department in which the faculty may be focused more on teaching than performing, it is also a good idea to bring guest artists to campus for your own collaborative work. These visiting artists can also provide small departments with much-needed "new information" from the outside world.

If you have a penchant for grant writing, the college or university environment can be a terrific place to start. Most colleges and universities function as nonprofit organizations. You may occasionally get funds from the departmental coffers but your best bet is grant writing. The beauty of this is that you bring the entire financial machinery of the college or university to bear upon your application. Plus, the institution manages the grant! There is rarely any competition across campus for grants in the field of music since, especially in the liberal-arts setting, there are few who apply outside the discipline. The college or university will actually help you write your grant proposal. Start locally and eventually expand to the regional or national level. Work with the grant-writing professionals in the office of development on your campus. Be prepared to describe the significance and positive impact your funded project will have on your locale as well as the institution. First, however, review the grant-writing guidelines in Chapter 6!

Regarding the world of college or university grant writing, there is one cautionary point. In higher education, the grant writer that works with you should be reasonably conversant with your discipline, highly qualified, and with a history of many years of successful grant writing. There is nothing worse than handing over your cherished projects to someone who is uninformed or inexperienced. Schedule an interview with your institution's grant officer. See if your project proposal is welcome and find out whether or not you will have a favorable partnership with the staff. Be sure to check on their grant-writing track record. This can save you time and heartache.

Lastly, if you choose to apply for a grant using the institution's nonprofit status, then where you may apply will be firmly determined by the college or university. This has to do with the larger fundraising campaigns set forth by an institution. It may be that your most important potential project funder has already been earmarked for a larger donation to the college or university. For all grant applications, you will be required to receive administrative permission in order to avoid a conflict of interest with the larger financial campaigns of your institution. That's true even if you decide to go it alone and write as an individual candidate. You want to avoid being in competition with your institution for financial support from the same foundation or granting agency. Again, your best bet is to find those grant sources that are committed to funding specific projects in the music profession.

Depending upon your project, you may want to also consider the world of "grants to individuals," or even to form your own nonprofit entity. As long as you are not competing with your institution, this can be an additional source of support. There are many sources available to the individual and your reference librarian can be an excellent adviser in your online search for access to these listings. Keep in mind that no database is comprehensive. There is considerable homework involved in finding just the right funding source for your worthy projects.

WHAT PRICE GLORY?

It's a rosy picture I have painted and for those artists who can straddle the professional world and the demands of academia, it can be a marriage made in heaven. It can also be otherwise. For some, there are serious challenges in joining these two worlds and important issues to consider in making the choice to work in academia.

Part of my work as a consultant has been in the area of assessment for college and university music departments. I have had the pleasure of visiting many types of institutions, working with faculties in their tenure and promotion review process, departmental ten-year assessment, curriculum development, and student portfolio evaluation. There are commonalities in all music departments whether they are small or large, urban or rural, public or private. Consulting brings you up close and personal to what challenges are present in this most lofty of professions.

For most institutions, the common challenge involves departmental politics. One can't write about higher education without mentioning this "elephant in the room." It permeates the ethos of a program, and often determines success or failure. What's the difference between higher education and the corporate world? In higher education they fight over nothing. I appreciate this humorous anecdote because it does remind us as artists that office space, rank, and on-campus notoriety are often ways that faculty seek validation and credibility. Once you are in academia, the measure of what you do as an artist may not even be evaluated by people whom you consider credible in your professional field. I recall one client's disturbing story of a colleague in a small Midwestern university music department who not only received a teaching award from the administration but was given this citation despite their well-known harassment of students and little professional work outside the university.

Artistic incompetence rarely lasts in the professional world, however. In the "real world" of the performing arts, one is measured over time by presenters, audiences, critics, and independent funding agencies, and often reviewed by national specialists in your field. The market place has diverse, independent, and detached assessment. If the concert doesn't go well, you probably won't be invited back. If you are abusive and authoritarian in your master-class teaching you most definitely won't be back. If you were inept at running a nonprofit, you will probably be fired. The real world can respond swiftly and bluntly to incompetence. This may be why many music departments and schools of music now regularly utilize independent reviews as part of the process for tenure and promotion. It's an idea whose time has come.

In the music profession, it's not unusual to find inflated egos and even a sense of entitlement. The truly great artists, however, don't go there. These rarefied professionals are at the top of their game, are eager to share their artistry, and are willing to provide mentorship to those coming up in the ranks. These luminaries are not bogged down in the petty distractions of competition or entitlement. They know that careers are built on hard work, talent, and luck. Gratitude and humility are part of their language and because time is a most precious commodity, they avoid wasting energy in negative pursuits.

Most of us in the course of our academic careers will deal with colleagues who are anywhere from mildly annoying to downright unsavory. You may encounter anger-management issues, professional jealousy, competition for in-house resources, petty fiefdoms, or even overt rancor. Depending upon the mix of your faculty and the size of your program, it can be very challenging to avoid being affected by the negative pursuits of others. And once people have tenure, it requires an enormous effort on the part of administrators to prevent bad behavior or professional incompetence. Tenure is most often a job for life and frequently allowances are made for varying degrees of ineptitude.

Nevertheless, if one is to survive in academia, there are a number of crucial issues that need to be addressed. To assume that your artistry alone will carry you is to be dangerously naïve. To assume that your good will, your excellence in teaching, and your genuine concern for the next generation of musicians will carry you to tenure is, at best, foolhardy. No one may care and no one (who is actually informed) may be listening. Your tenure dossier is one of the most important documents you will write and all manner of evidence must be corroborated. For example, you may have to explain why producing a commercial CD is a form of publication. You will definitely have to give evidence of your research regarding any recordings. In the area of performance, you will need to provide comprehensive concert listings at the national and international level. No one may be excited if you play even the Liszt Sonata locally. If, however, you do a joint recital with George Winston at the Super Dome, that's fodder for tenure. Additionally, your media coverage is important to include, and in great detail. There is no "small publicity" and as a collection, it gives a comprehensive picture of professional activity and excellence. Performing artists often have regular and at times spectacular coverage in print media, online sources, and through radio and television. It is well worth spending time developing those contacts. These activities support your career, and colleges and universities can't buy that kind of publicity.

While you are engaged in higher education, it is still important to remember that your job there is not your career. Your academic post is part of your career; it is simply one of the things you do. Often I consider my college employer as one of my clients. This goes along with what most investment counselors will tell you about money—don't put it all in one location. The same goes for your other valuable asset—your time. This also puts you in a position in which you need very little from the college or university—certainly not professional recognition and even perhaps not entirely money. Not needing something puts you in a position of power.

In addition to teaching, service, and professional activities, the tenure or promotion assessment should determine the candidate's ability to collaborate with departmental colleagues. The burden of proof will be on the candidate, no matter how dysfunctional the department.

All assessments ultimately stem from a clear and precise job description. I encourage music professionals to work in partnership with administrators to spell out in detail what is expected in terms of the tenure or promotion review. It's a good idea to check in annually with your department chair even if this is not built into your review system. Be sure to address those three competency areas.

TENURE ASSESSMENT COMPETENCIES

Teaching
Service to the institution
Professional activity

As I mentioned earlier, the issue of professional activity can be complicated. I suggest that you ask for a list of acceptable activities and a minimum number of performances or presentations needed for tenure. Whenever possible, it is to your advantage to qualify and quantify what the institution expects from you. Your department chair and academic dean can give credence to this template and as a result, you will have more precise guidelines as to how you allocate your time and resources on that tenure quest. Be sure to get all things in writing! Administrators come and go. Here is a sample model.

As part of her professional assessment, Jane Doe may choose from a combination of solo, chamber music, concerti, or collaborative public performances.

This might also include a summer music festival, residencies, workshops, or clinics. Ideally, she should give some of these performances or services at the national level and at least one performance a year should be on the campus of the college/university. Faculty-performance collaboration is encouraged. A minimum number of eight to ten performances per calendar year would be required, not necessarily of all different programs.

You may wish to include a commercially issued CD as professional evidence for tenure review. Unless you are producing a recording on a "vanity label," there is keen oversight in the market place on what companies are willing to produce. Quality is the first measure, however. There are many fine labels available to emerging artists and the costs can be manageable. A commercial recording can provide juried oversight to your work. Appearing on YouTube will not provide this critical evaluation for a tenure committee.

Don't overlook grant funding for a recording project, especially if you are looking to feature an underserved composer. A recording also provides an opportunity to receive additional outside evaluation in the form of reviews, professional assessment by national colleagues, and the recording company, all during the tenure process. While it can seem overwhelming to consider a full-time teaching load, service to the institution, and the myriad of professional activities that must be arranged, it can be a fairly simple project to produce a recording if you incorporate that repertoire into your regular performance schedule.

The tenure candidate and the department chair can also create a list of goals and projects for each academic year that would be keyed to the teaching load of that particular year and would be part of the tenure review. A timeline should be attached. Meeting with the chair of the department at least once a year can be helpful in underscoring the goals that are linked to the timeline.

Any tenure or promotion review includes an assessment of how a candidate balances professional and academic activities, is accountable for completion deadlines, and demonstrates his or her ability to consistently provide quality work. Overscheduling and unrealistic expectations can prevent candidates from doing their best work. They often request last-minute extensions. Fair and accurate assessment is difficult at best under these circumstances. Most institutions want to see evidence of how a tenure candidate is committed to the process of excellence. The administration needs proof of how well the candidate sets reasonable goals within the balance of teaching, service, and professional activities. Tenure and promotion candidates have an advantage if they set good personal boundaries, with realistic timelines accompanied by high-quality work.

The candidate who is a good fit with most music departments is the professional who is committed to teaching and genuinely enjoys students and the educational process. Ideally, this is an artist who has a real passion for teaching. Tenure evaluation also includes assessment regarding the likelihood of continued achievement once tenure is awarded. The candidate who is passionate about teaching and has a viable thriving career outside academia will be a successful contender for tenure. Commercial recordings and performances, juried publications, and outside media coverage can indicate that the candidate is a committed and talented performing artist, one who will continue to pursue a successful career long after a tenure award. This is crucial. As I mentioned earlier, the best fit for both institution and artist is to hire professionals who have a larger career outside academia. The academic post is simply part of that career. Administrators in today's higher-education environment ultimately want to see evidence that suggests the candidate will continue to distinguish him- or herself as an artist or scholar and teacher once tenure and promotion have been achieved. A larger career beyond the confines of academia is likely to ensure this.

Much of our discussion has centered on the process of acquiring tenure. If you are one of those musicians who is already ensconced in higher education, you may be considering your advancement to full professor. If you have been in academia for a long time, you may be faced with wanting to change career directions, revitalize your creative spirit, or even explore new musical frontiers. The three areas of competency required for tenure continue to be essential for any kind of promotion within higher education and so reviewing your own successful tenure process will give you clues as to how to proceed with your particular institution if you are looking for promotion. As for revitalizing your professional work, look to your own career, not your job in higher education. A career can span an entire lifetime and it may contain many varied jobs. For musicians who are experiencing soul loss in higher education or simply artistic ennui, this may be the time to return to crafting a new career vision. As I mentioned in earlier chapters, the vision–plan continuum is one that an artist often revisits throughout their career. You might also reread Chapter 5 as a way to jump-start your renewal.

SURVIVAL OF THE FITTEST

If, after weighing the pros and cons, the substantial investment of time and money for a terminal degree, and the fact that you answer to a full-time employer, you still choose higher education, then great! You are most likely someone with superb interpersonal skills, a dynamic career underway, a passion for working with young people, and excellent personal boundaries. Most likely you will thrive. Higher education can be a kind of new Esterháza. Like Haydn, you will have opportunities to provide your institution with an extraordinary body of music, bring many performers and cultures together, and also find time for mentoring the next generation of music professionals. With a clearly articulated job description, an agreement as to reasonable timelines and professional activities, and senior mentoring and accountability, colleges and universities will have all that you need to build a successful partnership as a performing artist. Through this process, institutions can retain a fine artist/teacher who will contribute in diverse creative ways to the overall reputation of the institution. The artist in turn will find a rich professional setting where he or she can make a significant contribution as a musician and educator.

Another employment model in higher education is worth mentioning. Some artists prefer to take positions that are not on the tenure track but are instead salaried one- to three-year appointment with benefits, or the traditional adjunct position. For touring artists who have heavy professional schedules, these kinds of posts are ideal. They have much less in the way of committee work, no tenure hoops, and reduced engagement with institutional governance. The adjunct position is the least committed and although the salary can be lower, the time commitment is usually only for what you do in class. The balance between income and time commitment is something to consider and it directly relates to how you envision your work and lifestyle as an artist.

Lastly, if you are interested in innovation and you want to move a brilliant idea forward swiftly, ask for an exception or a temporary proposal to the established policy. Policy change in higher education usually moves at a glacial rate (before global warming!). For some, it may even be wise to ask for forgiveness rather than permission. If you find an artistic home in higher education, remember, think like an artist, act like an academic!

Chose a job you love, and you will never have to
work a day in your life.

—CONFUCIUS

9

TRUE-LIFE STORIES

CONFUCIUS WAS PARTLY right. He might have considered, however, "Choose a career you love..." For most professional musicians, the choice to follow a musical career is rarely a "choice." It is often something that they simply have to do. The desire to connect with music for many is akin to breathing. One of my colleagues expressed it in this way, "I can't not do it!" Because this motivation and creativity are fueled by desire, musicians are particularly qualified to think in generative ways as to how one crafts a thriving career. Truly there are an infinite number of professional paths in the music industry. For every musician there will be a unique vision and strategic plan to realize those heartfelt dreams and goals.

In writing about how musicians can create their own vibrant careers, I have chosen to include a chapter that explores real-world examples. I have selected eleven diverse music professionals who in many ways exemplify the best in inventive career strategies. From these true-life stories you will find east- and west-coast perspectives, communities as different as New York City and small-town America, varied musical interests, different educational backgrounds, and divergent artistic visions. These artists remain anonymous but the details of their fascinating stories can serve as models to others.

In these narratives, there is a common theme. Each artist had reached a transitional point in his or her life, resulting in a quest for a new career paradigm. They were seeking a path that would allow them to live out their inner dreams and goals. For these courageous artists, the tipping point for change involved some sort of "last straw." Whether they had arrived at a dead end in their current work, changed geographic locations, or personal circumstances had shifted, each of these artists was motivated to seek new professional opportunities and to discover a renewed sense of vitality and joy in their work.

In these true-life stories, you will encounter musicians who have gone on to thrive in their endeavors. Each is making a living in their chosen field. These artists are engaged in a number of jobs: teaching, performing, grant writing, fundraising, arts management, consulting, among other activities. Most are midcareer professionals who encountered dissatisfaction in their work. Their stories offer examples of how artists can make effective career shifts, include new methodologies in their professional work, or seek more personally satisfying frontiers within the music industry.

It's easy for us to talk about the superstars in the music industry—that rarified cadre of artists who primarily perform, have major management, and pull in at least a six-figure income. Their careers are dazzling, high-profile, and seductive. Who doesn't want a musical career cared for by others? The music industry, however, is mostly inhabited by those countless professionals who remain under the radar screen of superstardom. Many of these specialists are able to make a comfortable living in a profession that gives them validation and purpose, not to mention great contentment. Their stories can serve as models to others wishing to thrive in the music industry.

In presenting these varied true-life narratives, I have chosen a format that presents both the artist's personal story as well as my own commentary regarding their place on the vision–plan continuum. I have included information about how each artist came to a career paradigm shift and what strategies they incorporated. Each story brings the reader into present time with these music professionals. As you read these narratives, see if you resonate with anyone in particular. Are there tips as to how you might discover your own artistic vision? For the planning process, do you find useful strategies for your own career? Perhaps you are looking to build an effective business model with realistic timelines. Maybe your challenge is with marketing. Possibly you need additional skills, requiring continuing education. Perchance you simply need to identify where you are on the vision–plan continuum. Each of these personal narratives has something to offer. In listening to these iconoclastic musicians you will undoubtedly find inspiration and guidance.

My first story begins with a woman I will call Maria. She is one of the most intriguing professionals I have encountered in the past twenty years. In her late twenties, Maria was a recent graduate of a liberal arts program with a Bachelor of Arts degree in English but also just a couple of credits shy of the music degree. By then, she was a published author with several novels to her name as well as numerous articles for various regional and national magazines. Maria had also had a short stint as the music critic for a small town newspaper and even worked briefly in the marketing industry. In addition to her many accomplishments, she was an experienced and talented pianist.

Maria played at an advanced level and had already performed in public for many years. It was during her return to private piano studies that she made a life-changing decision. Although she was eager to venture into new repertoire, to develop her technique, and to expand her local piano studio, she continued to experience considerable frustration at having to choose between her two professional passions: being an accomplished artist/teacher and a successful author/journalist.

As her professional career unfolded, Maria realized that she was indeed a kind of "hybrid"—someone who had genuine talent in two areas. Maria faced a common challenge that many multitalented artists encounter—how to successfully meld diverse talents into a career schematic. Of course if Maria were living in the nineteenth century, this would not be an issue! But in today's world we know that creative disciplines are often compartmentalized. For evidence of this, check out the catalog of most liberal arts colleges where you will find very specific requirements for highly structured majors in art, music, theater, film studies, and the like. Few colleges or universities offer a multidisciplinary approach to the arts.

As Maria entered her thirties, she began to reconsider how she saw herself as an artist and she resisted the temptation to choose "either/or." She had discovered that in order to move forward in a more satisfying and authentic career, her new artistic vision would need to include all of her skills and passions.

Instead of choosing either writing or music and settling on one full-time job, Maria went on to find ways of combining both her artistic pursuits. She turned her attention to developing "streams of income" and to look in many locations for professional activity. Since Maria had worked briefly as a marketing specialist, she had the necessary skills and chutzpah to promote her work. Moreover, she was an experienced entrepreneur. The results were amazing. Over the course of several years she expanded her work in the following ways:

1. Designed and administered a new concert series for living composers, featuring local and regional talent along with showcasing new music;
2. Developed an artists' series at her home church;
3. Formed a four-hand duo and toured regionally;
4. Wrote regularly for a number of music journals;
5. Acquired an adjunct teaching position at a local university;
6. Designed and wrote the website copy for a local music department;
7. Produced four commercial CD recordings, one featuring the works of a living composer;
8. Expanded her private piano studio;
9. Formed a "cabaret" show with a local singer;

10. Completed a Master of Music degree;
11. Received a national award in music journalism;
12. Volunteered her time to MTNA and the profession as well as for charitable nonprofits such as Meals on Wheels;
13. Established regular tithing of performances each year—playing for free or for reduced wages when she identifies a cause that needs her support;
14. Became editor of a professional music journal.

At the time of writing, Maria may be looking to academia as an ideal environment to combine all of her diverse experiences and education. Offering her work as a writer in service to her love of teaching could prepare her nicely for a job in academia. She could continue her work as both a writer and musician, but more importantly she would also have the chance to mentor music majors who may be favoring a career in writing as well! Maria is well positioned to continue her successful freelance life, knowing that each cell of her professional work is thriving.

Maria utilized her talents in marketing to advance her own career. She has gone on to share these skills as a consultant with other musicians interested in putting together their own publicity materials, press releases, and high-quality professional materials. Her work as a teacher has thrived with all that she is able to bring to her students. Maria has developed many successful partnerships and consortia with others: a church, a music store, a local university, regional MTNA chapters, music colleagues, regional chamber-music partners, and local businesses. She has created "streams of income" rather than searching for a single institutional supporter. Through her personal journey she discovered a new vision and developed a plan for her work. She describes her vision in her own words:

> I learned to take the music seriously and to show up, body and soul, for the music; to expand my view of music from a monolith of unattainable perfection to the discovery that it was a process; to realize that I had a right to play, and that I had a contribution to make to the world of music; to continue to inspire people with my love of music; and to give people two things: the knowledge that they are not alone, and the language and gift of music.

Maria began her transformative journey through first becoming aware of her own inner frustration at how she was working. In essence, she was at the very beginning of the vision–plan continuum. Her keen assessment of what gave her joy and passion served to point her in the right direction, however. She loved writing, performing, teaching, and being "out in the world." She knew that resolving her inner sense of frustration would somehow include utilizing all her talents.

Maria was also able to accurately acknowledge her real gifts and talents, those qualities that defined her. Drawing upon her diverse skills, Maria discovered that her career path would be unique. What defines her also makes her one of a kind in the market place. Having discovered the value of her distinctive interests and talents both in and outside the music industry, Maria continues to thrive in her professional career, living out her dream of working between two worlds: music and writing.

The next artist narrative deals with Barbara, a thirty-year veteran in the music industry. When Barbara decided to answer the call for change, she had already established a vital and successful career as a private piano teacher. Additionally, her personal background is rich with multicultural experiences. Having lived in Central America, she is bilingual in Spanish and English. During her childhood, she had for a time lived in the South Pacific. Barbara had a Master of Music degree in piano performance along with much of the accredited training to be a Suzuki piano teacher. When she and her husband relocated across several states to a college town of some 50,000 people, Barbara knew intuitively that it was a new opportunity to recreate her career. Barbara's initial challenge, however, was how to transplant her successful teaching business into what she perceived as a flooded market. Not only was this an isolated community, about two hours from the nearest metropolis, but it was also saturated with piano teachers.

The move to this college town also sparked new passions for Barbara. She had long wanted to return to her work as a performing artist and perhaps the move could open fresh opportunities to renew that part of her creative life. Although she had continued to perform over the life of her teaching career, she wanted to explore new repertoire, expand her technique, and venture into performing venues that had previously been unavailable. She was ready for a transformative experience. As an aside, artists can commonly be faced with what appears to be one or two pressing issues. Often, however, those singular motivations for change are simply the tip of the iceberg, revealing much more in the way of a desire for personal expansion.

Barbara was a candidate for deep transformation. Because of the self-imposed move to a new community, she had a ready-made opportunity for a fresh start and the chance to reinvent herself! Clearly that moment in time was a serendipitous opportunity to revisit her artistic vision. Although she had been engaged in a highly successful teaching career, she wanted to recast how she would meld that pursuit with other facets of her creative life. She was no stranger to the vision–plan continuum, having thrived in the profession for decades. Barbara's renewal was one of returning to her process with a new amalgam of goals. Building on her previous success (her "finest hour") and her own soul's desire, she brought to her new vision those additional artistic pursuits that would allow her to live more authentically. Since she already had experience in putting together a successful business strategy, she moved quickly in the implementation of her plan.

Sometimes changing geographic locations can provide just the right impetus for renewed creativity. Barbara was able to avail herself of many opportunities in her new community. A college town she discovered can, after all, be a great source for students, even though there may be an abundance of piano teachers already in the area. Faculty and staff from colleges and universities often encourage arts education for their children and are seeking an experienced, professionally trained teacher. Although her new locale was glutted with piano teachers, there was, in fact, no one who duplicated her training and experience. From this information, Barbara began to see things differently.

Since most public schools across the United States have made cuts in music programs, it's not unreasonable to assume that there are probably many eager parents and children looking for a highly qualified private music teacher. Barbara identified this need and built on it. The fact that she was able to capitalize on her bilingual skills and her Suzuki certification only added to her marketability. She focused on marketing her unique education, her extensive international experience, and her multicultural background. She reassessed her professional persona, leaving nothing to chance, being mindful that all her professional materials should reflect the high standards of her work—brochures, website, contracts, even wardrobe. She disseminated her first-class materials to both the public and private sectors of her new community: schools, civic organizations, religious centers, arts councils, and even the local newspaper. She was successful in garnering a feature story in the local paper regarding her multicultural background as a new resource for the community. Connecting with the local MTNA chapter was a "must" and she surmised that perhaps she could offer to share her Suzuki resources with others. Barbara also decided to participate in her state MTNA activities, taking on several positions of governance.

For the expansion of her performing career, she targeted a music festival that had a four-day master class for pianists. The master class was designed for teachers who made performance a regular part of their professional work. Performers chosen for the master class were automatically featured in an evening recital that was open to the general public. That program was not only part of the festival's concert roster but it also had significant media coverage in the local paper. What better way to be "seen and heard" than in a summer festival located in a prestigious venue? Barbara's audition was successful and she was chosen for the master class and, as they say, the rest is history. Through her festival experience, she had a chance to find out what she could do in a rigorous environment, she made connections with other professional artist/teachers from around the country, and she experienced much joy in returning to her love of performing.

At the time of writing, she is continuing to expand her repertoire, she has several chamber music groups that she regularly performs with, she has done numerous benefit concerts for a number of regional nonprofits, and her private studio is thriving. She is now turning her attention to a recording project of Latin American composers and she successfully completed the last levels of her Suzuki training. Concurrently, Barbara has also taken on various leadership roles within the governance of her state MTNA organization, and she continues to mentor young people as they begin their musical journey. Barbara is no longer the newcomer to her local music community but is now a well-known and highly regarded asset. As part of her outreach, she welcomes new professionals to her locale and shares with her colleagues her passion and expertise regarding the Suzuki method. She continues to add appealing works to her repertoire and includes performance opportunities as both a soloist and with colleagues from around the region while saving time for benefit work with regional food banks.

On the vision–plan continuum, it appeared, at least initially, that Barbara was looking for clarity regarding an aspect of her "plan." How would she launch a successful teaching studio in a new locale? What began as her initial exploration regarding marketing and development of her teaching in a new town quickly moved to the realm of her artistic vision. What Barbara discovered early on in her process is that in order to relocate her business to a new market place, she would need to revisit her artistic vision, one that would include an expansion of her work as a performing artist. Her plan, in order to be effective, would need to reflect that new artistic vision. She discovered that what had been useful for the past twenty years or so was no longer viable. Barbara's paradigm shift began with a sudden geographical change. From her career exploration and the work she did around crafting a new artistic vision and making a corresponding business plan, she was able to achieve a number of goals over the span of some three years. Those goals included:

1. Perform with greater confidence;
2. Strengthen and expand technique;
3. Fill in the gaps in knowledge of repertoire: primarily Baroque and twentieth-century performance practice;
4. Improve understanding of musical structure, harmony, and style;
5. Access publications of advanced jazz repertoire and also the tango music of Astor Piazzolla;
6. Complete the Suzuki Teacher Practicum;
7. Expand her private studio and the income base it provides.

Her own commentary, however, says it best:

> The most important thing that I learned was *to believe in myself.* I now place a greater value on my time and the work I do. I am more inner-directed and remind myself to worry less about what others think. I have greater respect for the profession of music education despite evidence of its devaluation in society. Out of this respect I now screen prospective clients and hold my students to high standards. Today I acknowledge that I am not a teacher for everyone, and that is liberating.

Barbara is an inspiration to others. Her well-honed plan of action and her generosity of spirit to others in the profession reflect her thriving career. She has built a kind of community consortium in connecting diverse groups and businesses in service to music. Through these partnerships, she regularly creates performance opportunities for both music professionals and aspiring students in her locale, thereby enriching her community with live music. In expanding her love of music-making she also discovered a satisfying outlet for her own artistic vision. Incidentally, Barbara is also a breast cancer survivor and one of my personal heroes.

Turning to international considerations, our third artist offers much in the way of inspiration. Robert is an extraordinarily talented artist and in many ways this was his biggest challenge, getting caught up to his true gifts. He received a Bachelor of Arts degree with a concentration in piano performance from a mid-sized state university but was informed by his major professor to put aside any dreams of a performing career or a job in academia. Robert was told that he simply didn't play well enough. So once he graduated, he set about carving out a multifaceted array of jobs. For nearly ten years he managed a section of one of the leading bookstores in the United States, he ran a small concert series, he played jazz piano in clubs at night, had a few piano students, did some composing and arranging, and was for a time quite content with this setup.

Gradually, however, Robert became restless with his work life. He decided to find a piano instructor in order to explore new repertoire and to renew his connection with music study. Robert was interested in underserved women composers, unusual repertoire from the twentieth century, and with his considerable background in French, he was especially drawn to new voices from the Parisian scene. Those weekly piano lessons proved to be the catalyst for his career transformation and through his renewed musical study, he realized that there were many more facets of himself that he wanted to include in his career mandala. He was clearly ready for a change and he wanted adventure, travel, and additional education.

Robert was not sure as to where his expanding career interests might lead, but he learned to trust the process. For most artists, this is half the battle. For some, it can be daunting to enter into that unfolding path without knowing the outcome. Robert found it helpful to work with Angeles Arrien's "Four-Fold Way," particularly focusing on being open to the outcome. In Chapter 6, I presented Arrien's cross-cultural wisdom as a model for how we can move from the envisioning process to bringing spirit into action. By tapping into this model, Robert could see the importance of being "open to the outcome" of his work. If he applied his efforts through being present to his vision, paying attention to what has heart and meaning, and speaking the truth without blame or judgment, the right and proper outcome would emerge. He could trust that. Not only did he learn to "be open to the outcome," but the end result of his journey was both remarkable and in retrospect, inevitable.

Robert was also interested in discovering ways that he could meld his interests in women composers, new music, jazz influences, and additional language study in French. For Robert, all those interests were already together and waiting—in Paris! He worked out a plan to take a six-month "sabbatical" from his day job at the bookstore and to live abroad in the City of Lights. There, Robert could study piano, work on his language skills, immerse himself in the culture, and begin his research on French women composers. He would also connect with IRCAM (*Institut de Recherche et Coordination Acoustique/Musique*), Pierre Boulez's center for new music, and take advantage of the rich international jazz scene. Robert was already in a process of gathering information and experiences in order to be clearer about his future career plans. Much of his artistic vision was in place. He chose to further clarify that vision through action. He boldly threw himself into those pursuits that were truly his passion and he structured this experience through his six-month "sabbatical." On the vision–plan continuum, he was well ensconced in the envisioning process. He had a list of desires and dreams that were already well established. Real-world experience and exploration would hone those goals into a singular vision—one that would later fuel a dynamic professional plan. When there were moments of fear or anxiety, he was able to put them aside. Since he had worked at the bookstore for ten years, he was able to negotiate for a six-month leave without pay, for the purpose of "further education." In this way, Robert would have a day job waiting if he decided to return.

To fund the Paris trip, he also chose to utilize some personal savings and he looked to his credit union for a small loan. In the meantime, he tackled several appropriate grants and began to make contacts in Paris for part-time work. Robert knew that in order to move forward with a more vital career, he would have to invest in himself. An investment in oneself is always good business. Markets rise and fall but our talent, education, and experience can never be "repossessed." There is no bankruptcy regarding the wealth of our knowledge. As his confidence grew, Robert came to discover that in fact he was his own best investment!

During his stay in Paris, he also decided to keep a journal. With so much new activity, change of scenery, and stimulating experiences, there would emerge undoubtedly many fresh ideas and considerations for the next career step. This written record provided Robert with an account of his experiences while in Paris, as well as a source to share with others. Undoubtedly there would also be fodder for an excellent journal article.

Upon his return from his six-month sojourn in Paris, Robert decided that graduate study was the next step in his emerging plan. His Paris stay and the immersion that it provided served to coalesce his career plans. Graduate school would provide him with a more focused program of study, award him with additional credentials, and prepare him for the next stage of his career. Robert wanted to continue his work as a performing artist in both art music and vernacular repertoire and join that with his love of all things French. Once he landed in graduate school, however, other ideas and prospects were to emerge.

After much soul searching, Robert chose a small east-coast liberal arts college. There he was able to work with a faculty mentor who specialized in French women composers. Relying on his former career in the bookstore, Robert was also successful in landing an excellent job in the college library. Three years later, he completed his Master of Arts degree in music.

During the masters degree program, Robert also discovered new opportunities and mentors that led him to develop his compositional skills, renewing his earlier passion for this work. Upon completion of the master's degree and with the wind in full sail he then moved to New York City where he enrolled in the City University of New York. He was awarded a teaching assistantship in the doctoral program and in time he became a successful composer in the New York scene. What had been an earlier sideline flowered into a full-blown career activity. With one opera already receiving public acclaim through New York City Opera, Robert is expanding his work to include new compositions in the field of opera as well as other genres.

What is most moving about Robert's story is that he listened to his heart and had the courage to begin a process that had no clear "prize" and no precise destination. Clearly there was no way he could be absolutely sure of the outcome of his endeavors. Robert knew, however, that he needed to apply all his efforts to his career journey and that as he approached that important crossroads in his professional life, he would need courage, hard work, and imagination. Robert had always held himself to the highest standards and so he was thoroughly committed to the process and to his own integrity. It led him to places that he never would have dreamed.

As Robert followed his heart and pursued the professional opportunities that most interested him, as he experimented with living out his diverse talents and skills, and as he continued to hold himself to the highest standards, he eventually discovered that he did indeed have a worthy and attainable artistic vision. For someone like Robert, experiential learning brought him to his own paradigm shift. As he ventured forth following the threads of his interests, he discovered experientially how to put his dreams into motion. His artistic plan was built one step at a time, and from the discovery and wisdom that direct experience can provide.

Robert continued to pay attention to both his inner and his outer worlds. Through his own journey he discovered a number of personal truths. In his own words: "There were many important things I came away with, but one very important thing I learned was that there was no reason I couldn't do what I had dreamed about doing and that it would only happen if I drew upon resources around me."

Robert also met the challenge of setbacks along the way. From the discouraging misinformation he received in his undergraduate years about a career in music to the common challenges of work and finances, he surmounted obstacles with tenacity and grace. His artistic vision became the sight point in all his work and emanating from that source was the knowledge that he could make a viable career path. Today he is in the final months of a doctoral program, and he is applying to colleges and universities for a faculty appointment that includes composition and music history. Of course his performance skills, his knowledge of art music and vernacular repertoire, and perhaps even those six months in Paris, will make for a very attractive résumé.

Robert is by nature a kind and thoughtful person. He is keenly aware of how others have assisted him in his journey and he regularly volunteers for a number of organizations both in and out of the profession. His main objective in this work, however, is to mentor those who are new to the music industry, and to provide encouragement and inspiration to seasoned professionals when they encounter setbacks. Recalling the help he has received along the way, Robert is committed to lending a hand to others.

The next true-life story involves a rock musician named Shaun. When you first meet him, you will encounter a man with a ready smile, a warm handshake, and just the slightest southern drawl. His story as a music entrepreneur is remarkable and moving. I chose to include him in this book because his career has touched on so many facets of the music industry; he represents a vast portion of the music world that is interested in what we loosely define as "pop" music, and because he is now living his vision–plan. In many ways, Shaun demonstrates how the vision–plan works and how you reap the benefits of living this process. On the vision–plan continuum, Shaun is in what I would call a "harvesting" phase. He completed a long and at times arduous process of connecting with his inner vision and values, made a concrete plan, and is now living that dream.

Shaun was raised in a small rural community of North Carolina. His parents were amateur musicians and valued the arts. Early in his childhood, Shaun was surrounded with classical music, a liberal arts education, and music studies, including dance. In high school he gravitated to the proverbial rock band where he developed a love of composing and playing lead guitar, and he carried these passions into his college years. Because his family saw music as an amateur pursuit, however, Shaun was strongly encouraged to pursue a professional career in the sciences. Since he was naturally gifted in this area, he followed his parents' lead and graduated with a Bachelor of Science degree in zoology. Music was never far from his side, however, and during college his rock band became successful, eventually attracting the attention of a commercial recording label in New York City. From there the band put out an album and started serious touring including New York City, Philadelphia, Washington DC, Baltimore, and the eastern seaboard, eventually garnering a contract with a major indie label. It was during these heady days that Shaun also learned about marketing and distribution, something that would serve him in the years to come.

Like many musicians, Shaun had one foot in the music industry and one foot in a "day" job. Putting his science background to good use, he acquired a job in the corporate sector just as the software industry was about to explode in the early nineties. With a fierce work ethic, additional education in the language of software, and excellent people skills, he quickly rose in the ranks and was eventually offered oversight of essentially the Midwest for a leading national corporation. Meanwhile, he was touring with his band, writing songs, and living life in the fast lane, the very fast lane. Because he was highly valued in his corporate job, he was able to juggle all these various activities. As he tells the story, however, there was the "corporate Shaun" and the "musician Shaun," and they were about to collide. It was at this moment, as he was about to turn thirty, that fate intervened in his life. As his band was about to take off at the national level, dissent broke out regarding the right vision for the band and after eight years of touring, it suddenly disbanded. What he thought would be his true artistic vision and plan simply imploded.

The loss of his band as its trajectory was rising brought Shaun into close contact with his own sensibilities about the dichotomy that existed for him between his musical life and the corporate world he inhabited. He turned down the offer to manage the Midwest market for the software corporation and essentially remained in Raleigh-Durham for the purpose of, as he said, "figuring things out."

During the next year, Shaun turned to an earlier employment model, that of bartending. As he described it, in this job he didn't have to care deeply, he enjoyed connecting with people, and this work gave him the necessary break he needed in order to discover the next step in his life.

The issue of "care," however, reemerged after a year or so in Raleigh-Durham. While the separation from his earlier lifestyle was essential, he discovered in that year-long stretch that what he was missing was the feeling of caring deeply about something. As he described it, he had to discover how to care again. Continuing with his personal quest, he moved to San Francisco, played in various bands; tended bar, and eventually found his way to the Northwest. It was at this point that his vision began to emerge: start his own record label, build a consortium of partners with like-minded interests, support emerging bands, and discover new professional collaborations. He could continue to write songs, develop his own band, record, but also expand into the world of featuring new talent.

Shaun put this vision into play through a multifaceted plan. He relied on the business acumen that he had gained in the software industry in conjunction with his diverse experience in the music profession. In describing his mission, Shaun is clear about his goals. He wants to connect those bands that have real potential for success with online distribution, access on iTunes, concert tours, a consortium of supporting partners, and a successful recording. As Shaun discovered, "Bands have needs!" The caring component of his life returned.

Shaun's record label took several years to become profitable. During that time he also continued his sideline of bartending, eventually owning a highly success-ful bar with two partners, one of whom is a celebrated chef. He regularly features up and coming bands in his venue and both his record label and bar have been recognized nationally. Shaun's passion includes mentoring emerging talent and as he offers, "I help people find the information and how to use it." He also adds, "If you can write a winning hit pop tune, you have a much easier time of succeeding as a commercial band!"

Today, Shaun is thriving with his bar and record label. He has launched several important bands and his outreach now includes European artists. Giving back is a way of life for this innovative entrepreneur. When a band that he had formerly signed to his own label decided to go with a national label instead, Shaun put aside his own business and legal considerations and offered to broker the deal on behalf of the band, all at no cost. As he explained, that band needed help. In the role of maven or mentor, Shaun also regularly connects people in the industry with one another, offering tips about the business, encouragement to those who are just starting out, and sound advice about avoiding the rocky shoals of the music industry.

In looking back at the challenges and trials, the disappointments and dead ends that he encountered, Shaun knows his success today was built on those experiences along with his triumphs. As he said, "It's good to get your heart broken, to care deeply about something, to get somewhere with yourself. It's worth everything."

Thus far I have focused on musicians who have already entered the professional world. Their stories are rich and savory, offering much in the way of guidance. As a contrast, however, I also want to include an entrepreneurial artist who is in the earliest stages of his career, just completing his education. I included Bill's story because he is truly an inspiration to those young entrepreneurs just entering the music industry.

By the age of fourteen, Bill was already an accomplished composer, oboist, and pianist. He pursued his passion for music not in a major urban center but tucked away in a small west-coast fishing port, two hours from the closest university, and three hours from a major metropolitan setting. His story is one of imagination, daring, and sustained commitment to his art.

Throughout high school, and with supportive parents behind him, Bill traveled weekly to a university in the next county for private piano lessons. Each summer he attended a national composer's camp for gifted young musicians. Over the course of his high-school years, Bill advanced his piano skills and knowledge of repertoire. He received composition coaching from an array of professional musicians, all the while continuing to perform as an accomplished pianist and oboist. He also added the violin, guitar, and trumpet to the roster of instruments he played. Eventually Bill headed off to college where he completed a Bachelor of Arts degree in music with particular emphasis on composition. It was the right blend for this multitalented young man and because he had begun his work as a composer in high school, he left his undergraduate training with a substantial portfolio.

Bill developed many lasting friendships with his college peers and regularly exchanged ideas and performances with other budding composers. He took advantage of every opportunity during his undergraduate education. According to Bill, "I learned how to be a professional musician. I learned how to feel comfortable playing music and be able to get myself to that place in any setting on any instrument that I play; that is the most important thing I learned how to do. I have zero performance anxiety today, and I always feel prepared no matter what the musical task is, and if I don't, I know when to step down."

With this sharpened sense of professionalism, Bill set his sights on New York City and was accepted to City College of New York where he completed the Master of Arts degree in music and a Master of Music degree in composition, scoring for film and multimedia.

On the vision–plan continuum, Bill was well into his plan of action as early as high school. In his own words, "I wanted to be a professional composer and performer. While the overall goal has never changed, my methods and approach have. I always thought I would be a film composer, but it appears that I am finding other ways of doing what I want and that incorporate the performance aspect as well."

What makes Bill's story so interesting is that even from those early high-school years, his vision has remained fixed. Yet he has been able to follow a plan of action that is both highly focused and, paradoxically, flexible—responding to synchronistic and serendipitous opportunities in the outer world. This may be why he is working successfully in New York City where competition is fierce. Today, Bill is continuing to build his composition portfolio, to perform regularly, and to develop remarkable and innovative professional networks. His own words say it best:

> My goal is to be a professional composer and performer as it always has been. I have since altered my plans to focus more on what I actually want to do and what comes naturally to me. I have launched into other genres of music, primarily rock and pop, where melody writing is a better fit for me. I still apply a classical aesthetic to what I do, by writing full orchestral arrangements for songs. The piano parts are quite pianistic as well. When someone asks me what I do, I tell them that I am a symphonic rock artist. This immediately implies that I am a performer, orchestrator, and usually composer as well. Because of this, I have also found some work as an arranger for other artists, because everyone wants string parts on their album! I have devised a plan to make myself the primary performer of my music, so now instead of wondering when my next classical piece is going to be performed or who is going to play it, I am in control of when and where my music is played. By orchestrating all of my songs, this has also allowed me to network and perform with many orchestral performers who join my ensemble as guests from time to time. Living in New York City, one finds that there are always too many people trying to do the same thing that you are doing, so creativity and versatility are important. I tell songwriters and performers that I'm a composer and I tell composers that I am a songwriter and performer. I focus on my traits that separate me from other composers and performers, not just in general, but catering to specific situations as well.

Bill is in the early stages of his career but already his entrepreneurial skills, innate musical talent, and willingness to adapt are shaping his success. On his vision–plan continuum, Bill is deeply engaged in living out his unchanging vision. He is following his plan, and at the same time creating new strategies as opportunities arise. There is a quantum aspect to his life in that his observations in the present moment serve to alter and sculpt his concrete plan of action. He savors and responds to each new opportunity that comes his way. Living steadfastly from his own authentic vision, Bill has built an impressive list of performances and recordings.

Bill is by nature a kind and helpful person, sharing what he has learned with others. As he says, he teaches music theory to whoever wants to learn, purely for the love of the subject. And when friends need a helping hand, he often provides free arranging for an important musical project. The future is wide open for this gifted and enterprising young man.

Turning to the world of interdisciplinary and multicultural arts performances, my next story features Patricia. Like many midcareer music professionals she found herself longing to expand her work in new and exciting ways. As a successful performing artist and teacher, Patricia surmised that additional education would be the right track for discovering ways to reinvigorate her work. She chose to focus on pedagogy and curriculum development. Upon the completion of a Master of Arts degree in music she accepted a professional engagement in Mexico where she presented a week-long musical residency in a wellness spa! This included her work as a pianist, vocalist, educator, and cultural ambassador. It was from this experience that a new artistic vision emerged. As Patricia so vibrantly expressed it, "I had the time of my life combining performance, teaching, and travel. I knew I was ready to move my career to another level but I didn't know exactly what that would look like. I needed a fresh perspective. I was ready to work with someone who could help me analyze my experience, education, and talents and help me to put those to work as I moved my career to a new level."

Patricia knew that a dynamic change was her best bet in advancing her career. Her moving experience and connection with Mexican culture helped to coalesce her emerging artistic vision. Patricia also had a keen awareness as to what sparked her passion and interest. She wanted more of *that*. Interestingly enough, when Patricia approached her graduate-school adviser and later the director of the program, neither had the resources, nor did they direct her to anyone who would mentor her postgraduate planning. Patricia was disappointed and found it difficult to reconcile with the large amount of tuition she had invested in her graduate degree. Nonetheless, in true entrepreneurial spirit, she moved ahead, ready for change and new challenges in her work.

Patricia soon acquired an independent career consultant. She chose to work with this mentor at the beginning of her quest for a vision. On that vision–plan continuum she was on the threshold of articulating her goals and dreams. She clearly knew that she wanted a dramatic change from her earlier career and she was sharply focused on what components her new life would need to include. Patricia was highly motivated and had already laid much of the groundwork for crafting an exciting and authentic artistic vision.

Patricia's earlier professional activities had included running a successful piano studio and some ancillary work in teaching voice as well as guitar. As a professional pianist, she took the route of regularly performing for events, weddings, art museums, libraries, and local area music teacher gatherings. Patricia can improvise, play from a lead sheet, and play by ear. She has often used narrative when appropriate, and through the use of story she discovered that she was able to connect with audiences in fresh and invigorating ways. For Patricia, the traditional style of concert performance had left her feeling somewhat disconnected from the audience.

While combining performance with narrative, Patricia also began to explore the music of Mexican and South American composers. Her first project included the repertoire of Manuel Ponce. Given her near-bilingual skills in English and Spanish, she discovered new opportunities for performance in her regular venues as well as in schools. She had had experience in the public school classroom during her graduate work in curriculum development, and so an outreach to this population was obvious.

Patricia was passionate about diverse performance venues and wanted to develop her ideas of including narrative as well. She also wanted validation that her vision was something worth pursuing, given the fact that she had been trained in a much more traditional fashion. The work she did with her mentor helped to confirm and clarify her artistic dreams. As her vision became clear, she was able to develop a riveting plan of action. With her strong skills in website design, marketing, arts administration, teaching, performing, and touring, she was primed to be her own business manager as well.

Patricia moved into the "plan" phase of her work, as she so aptly described it, "at mach speed." Her whirlwind paradigm shift may very well have happened because she began her quest for a vision with considerable experience in the things that drew her passion and interest. She loved to perform and teach, enjoyed sharing her knowledge of music with wide-ranging audiences, found storytelling to be an exciting component to her presentations, and felt a sense of purpose and validation in intercultural connections. She was absolutely clear about what captured her attention, and because of this, she had already been exploring some of her new goals and dreams.

The following list charts Patricia's course over the nearly two years that she took to launch her vision–plan. She developed a business strategy, sought out the right professional advisers to assist her, and applied her organizational skills in the development of her own long- and short-term timelines. Her most innovative product, however, is her captivating array of programs, residencies, lecture recitals, story, and show. It all equals Chautauqua! Patricia drew upon the model of a late nineteenth-century summer institute in Chautauqua, New York, which offered the arts and humanities through lectures, performances, and story. Patricia discovered through her research that the Chautauqua model spread to hundreds of organizations around the

United States and by 1912 this commercial endeavor was a highly popular form of entertainment. Her own twenty-first-century Chautauqua has enjoyed artistic and commercial success. With her infectious enthusiasm and her personal mission of bringing music to underserved audiences, she is a superb model for any music entrepreneur. In Patricia's own words, "I went from being a private teacher who performs a little, to thinking and living as a music entrepreneur."

Here are some of the things that she accomplished during that two-year phase.

1. Created a business model with one, two, and five-year goals;
2. Developed an innovative product, including a Chautauqua style of performances and residencies;
3. Created an array of new marketing materials (printed materials, website);
4. Wrote press releases and travel articles that helped to secure future performance and residency dates;
5. Created promotional kits (electronic and hard copy);
6. Developed program and residency guides to accompany her Chautauqua presentations, leaving additional long-term classroom activities and discography and bibliographic resources for the presenter;
7. Presented performances and residencies in France, Mexico, and in the states of Montana and Washington;
8. Was listed on the juried roster of teaching artists for her local state arts commission;
9. Presented twenty Chautauqua performances in 2010;
10. Researched underserved Mexican and Latin American composers;
11. Continued to develop Spanish speaking skills;
12. Laid the groundwork with a commercial recording label for an all-Ponce CD;
13. Applied to showcase at regional booking conferences;
14. Booked next season's concerts.

As Patricia shifted into high gear with her new career plan, she continued to nurture her private teaching studio. She shares her ideas and tests curriculum in the lab of her own students. Her teaching schedule has become flexible to include her travel and performance activities, and because her students know she is an active professional out on the road making music, her waiting list has swelled. Her ongoing passion for both Mexican and Latin American cultures has inspired her to continue improving her Spanish speaking skills along with adding dance to her studies. Patricia's residencies may very well invite the audience to join in with the samba or merengue!

Like all thriving entrepreneurs, Patricia knows the importance of giving back to her local and regional communities. She regularly offers music residencies and performances in her daughter's elementary school. Recently, while on tour in Montana, she returned to her childhood community to provide two free performances for the local school district. And as a member of MTNA she mentors and encourages other professionals looking to create new career paths.

Speaking of interdisciplinary models, the next narrative presents Simone, a gifted performing artist and teacher who, following the award of a Doctor of Musical Arts degree, answered her longing to reconnect with her concert career. The final stages of a doctoral program can be for some very dry: preparing for the general exam, launching the dissertation project, and ultimately defending one's research. There are few hours left in the day for the kind of practice required for concert performances.

The conclusion of her doctoral studies gave Simone a ripe opportunity to return to her concert work. As she crafted her strategic plan, she also decided to keep her private teaching studio to a minimum in order to launch her performance initiative. She wanted to immerse herself in new repertoire, arrange for performances, go on tour, share music with diverse communities, and in particular, feature the music of women composers.

Having written her dissertation on an aspect of feminism in music, Simone was keenly aware of the wealth of music by women composers, spanning several centuries. Simone's brilliance was in evidence when she decided to team up with a gifted actress, bringing the lives and music of women composers to life in performance. She would develop a "show" around the stories of these extraordinary women and weave in performance samples of their music. It would be a vivid and experiential connection with lesser-known composers and it would give voice to their place in the evolution of music.

Simone's initial challenge was not crafting her vision. That was clearly in place. On the vision–plan continuum, Simone discovered that she was at the beginning of the planning stage. As she so aptly said, "Where do I start?"

What is instructive about Simone's story is that she already had in place her artistic vision. While this project may not have been the sum total of her future career plans, she nonetheless was passionate about creating this performance outlet and she intuitively knew that it would carry her in the direction she most wanted to go—resuming her concert career. She had carefully thought through her artistic vision, she trusted that her significant project on women composers would open doors to her performance career and that she could follow an aspect of her interdisciplinary interests in collaboration with a fellow artist.

Simone could actually envision the final product. She had a clear sense of the show with its music, costumes, written script, simple props, and the richness of interdisciplinary performance. Next, she had to consider what markets would be best for this kind of presentation. Like all clever entrepreneurs, Simone was looking for a "need" in the market place.

Simone knew that the topic of women composers had become very popular throughout the United States, particularly in the world of higher education. In the past twenty years, there have been a number of initiatives regarding gender studies, as well as greater funding resources for artist residencies that are interdisciplinary in nature. Simone had both topics covered! At the college or university level, Simone discovered that you are more likely to arrange for concert bookings and command your fee if you have several departments paying for your residency. If you have a high-quality press kit, educational materials, brochures, a dynamic website, and good phone skills, you can easily book the concerts yourself, even without professional management.

For most of the colleges and universities Simone targeted, she initiated her contact with the office of academic affairs. This type of administrative office often promotes and oversees interdisciplinary events on campus. It's a way that college administrators can include many disciplines in their funding and stretch their dollars further.

Simone also used her considerable writing skills to apply for a number of grants. Even though she was giving a performance, the interdisciplinary nature of her work and research qualified her for humanities support. Her proposal writing could dip into two funding sources: the performing arts and the humanities.

The colleges and universities that hired her were able to fund her "show" from several departmental budgets. In Simone's case, she attracted interest from such areas as music, gender studies, history, and theater. And because she held the DMA degree, she was highly credible to her fellow academics. As part of her residency, she could provide top-quality lectures in a variety of disciplines.

Within six months Simone had her materials ready to go, her website up, a show developed, and bookings in hand. Her greatest market was, not surprisingly, the small liberal arts college. I had the pleasure of seeing one of her exquisite shows. Everything was there in full rainbow strength: her vision, high-quality, superb preparation, and engaging delivery. It's hard to predict where this artistic project will take her. My guess is that with her innate talent and imagination, she will discover serendipitously new and exciting performance frontiers.

My next true-life story is about Louise, a young woman who first trained as a classical violinist. Her story is a moving personal account of how she came to follow her own personal artistic vision one step at a time, really one awareness at a time. An explorer by nature, she used those experiences and her powerful intuition to discover what she really wanted to do as a musician. By her own account, that process to discover her vision took some ten years. In an interview for this book she spoke with passion and insight. I have chosen to present her story using many of her own words.

Louise began classical violin lessons just after her fifth birthday, after watching a group of children play violin. Her teacher regularly incorporated fiddle music into the more traditional curriculum since their local mountain community favored this folk idiom. From there, Louise moved to a more rigorous course of study some three hours by car from her home. Those early years of study were, as she describes, "The beginning of a long journey toward finding myself in the big world." Her new instructor was a Suzuki-trained teacher who believed in dedication and focused practice. She inspired Louise to listen carefully to what she was playing. Louise adds, "The classical violinist inside me was being trained here."

During high school and college, Louise led summer wilderness trips. With the aid of domesticated llamas, she escorted campers from around the world into the remote regions of her locale. She notes, "I took my violin into the mountains and canyons to play for the guests by firelight. In reflection, this regular use of music as a tool for storytelling and community would sprout more ideas."

Louise's plan upon entering college was to be a psychology major with a minor in music. She was awarded a number of music scholarships, however. As she began her university studies, she had important confirmation that music must be an important part of her emerging adult life. Still, she wasn't sure about how to make a living from music. That path was not clear. Things began to shift, however, once her college studies were underway. Her psychology adviser didn't show much interest in her, particularly when Louise found herself floundering in the large general-psychology classes. With her music studies thriving, she decided to move to the music major course of study, and subsequently graduated with a Bachelor of Arts degree with a double minor in psychology and theater. Meanwhile, during her freshman year, she had also opened her own violin studio for students in preschool through fourth grade. Initially, her motivation to take this entrepreneurial step was for extra spending money, but quickly Louise discovered how much she enjoyed getting to know her students and their families. Inspired by these teaching encounters, she eventually went on to write her senior thesis on how children benefit from music instruction.

College life presented many challenges. On the one hand, Louise and her music adviser worked well together. Louise was able to explore new goals, experiences, and dedicate more time to her musical education. On the other hand, her violin teacher proved to be harsh, discouraging, and not the least bit interested in folk music of any kind. Louise found herself moving away from the violin and with that came turmoil. She posed new questions to herself, ones that were the first seeds of a new artistic vision. "Who was I as a musician? What music did I want to play? What music would I play? How would I change lives with music?" The answers to these life questions did not come quickly and so over the course of many years Louise traveled, shared music (both classical and folk) with a host of divergent cultures throughout the world, and continued to teach violin to children. Life was on the move for this young musician, and she was able to live in a number of communities throughout Central America as well as expand her work to many rural and urban areas throughout the United States.

Eventually settling in the Northwest in her late twenties, it was at this point that Louise encountered a superb Suzuki teacher/trainer. She signed up for a two-year apprenticeship and her future began to open wide. Through this program of study, Louise had a life-changing experience, remarking that, "My teaching tools grew tenfold and I now have a deeper understanding of the Suzuki method. I compare this method to a way of living versus solely a method to learn the violin."

Louise discovered in that journey from childhood to early adulthood that she did indeed have an undeniable passion for teaching children. As she sees it, many of her educational projects for youth have been reseeding music as a tool to build community and relationships. Through many years of volunteer work with underserved communities and through the jobs that she pursued, Louise encountered those experiences that spoke to her heart. She offers this insight: "I am still finding my musical self and accepting that fiddle music is just as valid a form of musical expression as classical music. It speaks to me, moves me to my bones. Teaching comes naturally to me and is rewarding. Teaching gives me a chance to know families and relationships, as I would have as a psychologist. And the Suzuki method truly is about living a noble, kind life. So I teach a fusion of the Suzuki method and fiddle."

Louise knows her true artistic vision. Today, she is on the midpoint of the vision–plan continuum—just beginning the plan phase. My guess is that with her clear vision she will sculpt an innovative and dynamic plan.

Louise has acquired a new level of wisdom about who she is and what her artistic vision is. She offers this insight.

I am still discovering myself through music on a daily basis, working to loosen that creativity and let it flow. To know that what I love is enough, that the music that stirs me, that weaves through my early morning dreams is my music. And that is enough. I am getting to know myself through music. It's a journey. And I am building community and relationships through music. Music making is my own internal psychologist—if I show up every day, practice, sit in that comfortable chair and talk with my "psychologist," growth and joy will follow. I have given myself an open invitation to explore all musical styles, particularly cultures where music is still deeply interlaced into the tapestry of daily life. I am keeping music teaching as my career but tailoring it, accepting what I like and dislike. Today I focus on using music as a way to nurture relationships within families and communities. Start small, with me. And grow to reach others.

For Louise, the border between work and philanthropy is fuzzy. Since much of her artistic vision emerged from the volunteer sector, she has continued these activities as part of the fiber of her professional life. Today she assists at a local public school with a new pilot project for first through fifth grade: Fiddle Club. It has taken off and parents have stepped forward to support the continuation of this extracurricular activity. In the area of private teaching, she regularly offers creative exchanges to students and families who cannot afford those lessons. Sometimes it is with a professional trade such as helping with media projects and even language tutoring. Whether Louise is following one of her professional streams of income or engaged in her volunteer outreach, it's about building community and relationships through music. As she begins to launch the focus and direction of her career, she will undoubtedly rely on the wealth of experience and wisdom that she has acquired, knowing that with a clear artistic vision she can make that business plan, craft those strategic timelines, and find new professional collaborations.

My next true-life narrative presents Cynthia, an entrepreneur who discovered ways of building her career through interdisciplinary channels. She is a remarkable inspiration for how we can live as music entrepreneurs who intersect with other disciplines, even those far afield from music.

Cynthia's story begins with the traditional study of music in childhood. At a young age she was captivated by the sound of the viola and after many years of serious study, through the conservatory level, she garnered a Bachelor of Music degree in performance, eventually landing a position as a violist in a major American orchestra. For some eighteen years she lived her dream of having a full-time orchestra job. As she described, "I loved the way playing in an orchestra made me feel, and that's what I wanted to do for a living!"

Cynthia settled into the routine of orchestra work, and for many years she found community and collaboration in a way that was personally satisfying. Gradually, however, she discovered that in fact, she had many more untapped professional interests and various facets of herself that were not being expressed or explored. Although she loved making music and performing to a high standard, she knew that there was something beyond this realm that would fulfill her longing.

On one particular airline flight, fate would intervene. During the course of this flight, Cynthia encountered an abusive man harassing a woman to the extent that he could without other people intervening. As Cynthia describes: "I felt outrage in my body. Maybe this energy has something to do with my next step." This jarring experience stayed with her and upon her return to her daily orchestra schedule she began volunteer work for a women's domestic-violence hotline, soon discovering how passionate she felt about helping others in this way. Cynthia realized that in order to feel whole, she would need to expand the scope of her life's work. Her new sense of personal and professional vision emerged from what appeared to be a rather vague internal longing combined with real-world experiences. Her success in moving forward was directly related to her willingness to listen to her inner ideas and feelings. Those gut reactions and intuitive messages were key to her next step.

While maintaining her full-time orchestra position, Cynthia enrolled in a graduate-school program in psychology. She eventually became a licensed professional counselor with a master's degree in counseling and certification as a practitioner of psychodrama. As she said, "It was the most difficult transition of my life." This choice, however, allowed her to do what many artists desire—transpose in diverse ways one's gifts and talents, ever expanding a sense of self and outreach to the world beyond.

Today, Cynthia continues to perform regularly as a professional musician, although no longer within the confines of a full-time orchestra position. On her vision–plan continuum, her plan is underway. She is firmly engaged in the process of living gracefully between two worlds: therapist and musician. Although she has not achieved all of her goals, she knows that the path she has chosen is the right one. She can feel it. As she describes, "It's so worth it to stay focused on your intention and not let 'no' be the last word. Find ways to make it happen!"

In reflecting upon her journey to expand her professional horizon to include work as a therapist and performing musician, she offered this insight.

> There is an attitude I have encountered, perhaps this is in other professions as well, that if you aren't myopically devoted to one form, then you aren't serious about it, or [don't] deserve to be taken seriously. I believe that is short sighted, but [it] may allow some folks to feel safe. I love Yo Yo Ma's courage to bridge with other art forms. There can be great resonance within oneself and with others when we open up to expanding our sense of ourselves, our talents, and our roles.

Cynthia's work as a therapist is in many ways a form of giving back. By helping people to find their true calling and "essential self," she is able to enrich and heal the lives of many. Added to this is her volunteer work for hospice, women's crisis centers, and the rescue of women and children from dangerous domestic situations. Cynthia is a woman of many facets. From her richly textured life, she is able to bring wisdom and guidance to many. Cynthia crafted her vision through intuitive awareness.

She responded to her own inner wisdom about the need to live out other parts of her personality and talents. Her strategic plan included additional education, launching a new business model, and continuing her work as a stellar musician.

One of the things I most admire about Cynthia is her humility and humor. As she says, "I have been known to make ends meet as a street sweeper, egg flipper, security guard, switchboard operator, and nanny." She also rides a motorcycle.

For the next narrative, I chose to include Howard, a man in his late thirties, living the life of a thriving music entrepreneur. His life, however, did not always have such a clear trajectory. His story brings us up close and personal with the process of shifting careers, pursuing new educational tracks, and taking a leap of faith into the depths of his true personal vision.

Howard's story begins with childhood music studies on trumpet and piano. He participated in his high-school band program and continued to enjoy attending concerts. As he prepared to embark on his college studies, he acquired an acoustic guitar and from there, music continued to enrich his life. Along the way, he also developed an extensive record collection.

College brought a multitude of rich experiences and in Boston Howard graduated with a degree in communications including a specialty in photography. Through twists and turns of fate, however, he eventually fell into a steady job as a tax specialist, and for nine years worked successfully for a large chain of veterinarian hospitals throughout the United States. Nonetheless, as time went on, Howard found himself less and less willing to stay with his stable job. As Howard expressed, "Is this really all life is about? How did I get here?" Fortunately for Howard, he had the answers: "I got there by not choosing, and not following my heart." It was around that time that he discovered a new instrument, one that truly spoke to his soul—the fiddle. His future was about to open.

Sometimes musicians can craft their artistic vision and sometimes it arrives in serendipitous ways. Howard was the accidental entrepreneur in that one interest led to another. He simply had to follow his passion. Howard's keen interest in the fiddle prompted him to explore the instrument itself and how it worked. He had always enjoyed tinkering with things, working with his hands, observant of the minutiae. He loved to build things, repair a broken toy, or bring something back into usefulness. Gradually, Howard began to acquire an array of string instruments in various states of disrepair. But more often than not, he would have to resort to a luthier in order to fix them. This planted the seed for the next stage of his life. He wanted to be that luthier.

As Howard described, "Gearing your life to become a luthier is not easily enacted, especially by someone mired in an entirely unrelated endeavor for a decade or so. I thought that it wasn't possible for me to relocate geographically at the time, and directly approaching professionals in the business proved unfruitful. I was of no use to a luthier or violin shop without any training." Luck, however, intervened and Howard discovered a local violinmaker who would host him as an apprentice for several years.

In the long run, however, Howard knew that he would need to pursue a more structured approach to learning the luthier craft and so after concluding his apprenticeship, he packed up his belongings, quit his day job, and with his wife and dog, moved halfway across the country to complete a one-year technical training program which focused on the repair of violin family instruments, with an optional violin-construction component. Howard knew this training would be a foot in the door of the industry. Upon the completion of his studies, he relocated to the west coast and landed a job working in a violin shop. Howard offers this insightful narrative.

> I can genuinely say I love what I do. One of the most appealing things about this career, besides the enjoyment of the work itself, is the prospect of working for myself. I am learning quite a bit working in the shop, though I am anxious for the day I can be my own boss. I specifically chose the program that I did because it's an employable skill, but I also really enjoy building violins, and hope that I can do that also to some degree, if not solely. But I think the beauty of this work is that I will always be learning, and much of it is learning as you go. At some point I feel like I will be able to say, "Well, I know how to do 90% of what I'll be asked to do 98% of the time. I'll learn the other 10% on a need-to-know basis." I'm not there yet. I still have to eat Top Ramen noodles! So I have to pay my dues for a short while longer, but I am beginning the process of acquiring my own tools, networking with other luthiers and developing contacts with suppliers and dealers, building my inventory, registering a business name, thinking about good locations for my business, and most importantly, practicing my skills constantly. When I'm not working, I'm working on my own projects. I'm getting my hands on quality instruments whenever I can, and studying the history of the great violinmakers too. I've also befriended a professional violinmaker who is willing to help me.

Clearly, Howard is embedded in the "plan" stage of his process. He is putting together all the necessary components to realize his vision. What is inspiring about his story is that he chose to take this course of action in the face of a secure and lucrative job at a point in midlife. He also was lucky enough to have a supportive wife and family. Howard was able to connect deeply with his artistic vision and the heartfelt goals that motivated him. Howard is now living out his detailed business model for success, relying on collaboration and networking to expand his professional connections.

As with any thriving entrepreneur, Howard is readily giving back to his community and profession. He volunteers in local schools. He donates his skills, time, and materials to repair and set up many of the violins used by the students. And he plans to be involved with the nonprofit organization Luthiers Without Borders, with the hopes of offering his expertise to other locales in need.

Lastly, I have chosen to conclude this chapter of true-life stories with an artist whose life has spanned many decades. Richard is ninety-two years of age. His story reminds us that entrepreneurship and creativity have no age limit. And since this process of renewing one's vision and plan ideally recurs throughout a lifetime, Richard's story can light the way for all musicians as they enter their retirement years. As I quoted Dychtwald in Chapter 6, middlescence, or that period we have traditionally identified as "retirement," can be an expansive and fruitful time of life.

Richard was born in Duluth, Minnesota, in 1920 to Irish and Polish/German parents. Music and the arts were important components of everyday life and by the age of twelve, Richard had his first baritone horn. It was 1932 and the Great Depression was well under way. His father, a tuba player, showed him the basics and supported opportunities to play in local bands. In fact, when John Philip Sousa performed in Duluth, Richard's father was hired to perform with that select ensemble.

Fast-forward to 1937. Richard discovered that if he enlisted in the National Guard, he could receive a new state-of-the-art baritone horn. With that horn he auditioned for college and received a music scholarship as he embarked upon his program of study in engineering. In 1940, he reenlisted in the National Guard, but by September of that year all members of the National Guard were moved into the regular army and Richard left college for Fort Lewis in Washington state. Following the attack on Pearl Harbor, he was shipped to the South Pacific where he remained in combat for the duration of the war.

Throughout his army years, Richard played both baritone horn and trombone. He was part of an elite army band from the Forty-First Division. Upon his return to the United States, he resumed his education, married, had four children, and rose in the ranks of academia to become a dean in a school of education at a large urban university. Music was, however, a constant. If he wasn't launching his own "big band" then he was part of a local-area band. His talent and knowledge of the big-band repertoire put him in high demand and so for over three decades he lived in two worlds: educational administration and research, all the while pursuing the life of a freelance musician.

As Richard approached retirement, however, something shifted. In the late 1970s, conditions were favorable for many in academia to take early retirement. With this prospect, a new personal vision emerged. Like the skilled administrator he was, he knew he would have to make a strategic plan of action based upon his vision. Richard took that early retirement and built his second professional career, in music.

Beginning at age fifty-eight, Richard left academia for the full-time pursuit of music performance. He decided to put together essentially a regional big band. Drawing upon his leadership skills, his management and consulting experience, and some fifty years of performing as a musician, he launched his big band. With numerous contacts in the regional market, he was able to attract the very best talent. Supporting this venture, however, was the "book" that he would use. He hired a well-known and experienced arranger to produce a book of big-band arrangements for six-piece, nine-piece, and seventeen-piece bands. He was ready for any market! And since he regularly added to the book top-forty hits, he kept his material contemporary. Richard's vision was razor sharp, as was his detailed business plan.

With his well-established track record as a regional musician and with the superb arrangements in his book, he attracted the finest musicians for his ensemble. He produced a high-quality demo recording, excellent media materials, and shopped them around the region. Landing a few key dance clubs, hotels, conventions, and events, he gradually expanded his networking outreach. Richard's natural charm and love of music were great assets and so, along with occasional help from a local manager, he was able to perform, run the business, and book the performances. With attention to detail and excellence, he had regular repeat engagements. By his mid-sixties, he was up to nearly 100 gigs a year! The success fed on itself and with a top-flight ensemble and regular employment, he was able to tour the region and present the very best in big-band performance. It's important to note that Richard had grossed two million dollars by his twentieth year in operation. In a clever move, he also invited his daughter to join the ranks as the lead vocalist and electric bass player. Years later this was to prove fortuitous.

Until Richard was eighty-nine, he continued to play those regular gigs. With his daughter in the picture, he was able to turn some of the day-to-day business over to her. On his ninetieth birthday he performed all evening with his band, much to the delight of all in attendance. With a gradual shift from bandleader to band member, he continued his love of music performance, sharing with others the great hits from the big-band era and beyond.

Today, Richard lives independently with his wife of sixty-three years. He is still involved with his band, as his daughter has taken the helm. With his wealth of experience and knowledge, he is able to mentor her as she prepares to expand the outreach of the band. There is even talk of a big-band retrospective in France, joining French and American musicians in memory of the French liberation.

Richard's story tells us a lot about how to survive life's hardships and go on to thrive. The Great Depression and the Second World War were tremendous challenges to most Americans. Like many from that extraordinary generation, Richard not only went on to prosper but he also retained his zest and vitality in living with commitment and zeal. He knows that music is an integral part of who he is and he has never lost sight of that passion. Richard has woven music into the fiber of his life and at the moment of retirement he took full rein of a second full-time career—one that has spanned some thirty years.

As with most successful entrepreneurs, Richard has a long track record of giving back. His band has regularly performed free of charge for all kinds of services and events that he knows will be truly enhanced with music. For those worthy organizations in the nonprofit sector that are struggling with funding, Richard has also lent a hand in grant writing and development. Throughout his academic career he produced a steady stream of grant awards in the field of education. He has directed that skill and experience to aid nonprofit arts organizations. For this savvy entrepreneur, life continues to unfold in service and mentoring to others.

These true-life stories are a sampling from the much larger world of thriving music entrepreneurs. The artists shared their own personal journeys, showing how they responded to their own desire for change. They found themselves at a distinct point on the vision–plan continuum. Some of these musicians had work to do regarding the development of their vision, clarifying their dreams and goals. Others were challenged with the details of putting their plan forward, exploring new strategies and crafting an effective business model. And some were harvesting the fruits of their labor. Whether you are a performing artist, an educator, writer, one who works in the publishing or recording industry, or someone who is firmly ensconced in the nonprofit world, you can benefit from the vision–plan continuum. We make real what is first imagined.

There are many more stories to tell. You undoubtedly have your own. Everywhere you look, thriving musicians will have a tale of their own journey. The stories will be different but they will all have begun with a personal vision made manifest through careful planning. As you move forward in your career, look to what you do best, your "finest hour." Notice those pursuits that give you joy and seem effortless. What is in your heart, your true desire? What work leaves you at the end of the day alive with more energy? What is it that you most want to share with others? Can you identify where you are on your own vision–plan continuum? What is it that you need in order to move forward? In answering these questions, you will know if you are on the right track.

10

CONCLUSION

WITH EACH CHAPTER in this book I have focused on the various components that go into creating a dynamic and vibrant career in music. I have offered examples from the literature, wisdom from professionals in the field, and data from my own career as an artist and teacher. No book on the subject of music entrepreneurship can be fully comprehensive, however. This is due in large part to the fact that there is no one formula for success. We can only rely on guiding principles. If we are to create a thriving music career, we must discover our soul's desire, our unique mission in the world of music, our amalgam of talents and skills, and the innovative ways in which we can bring these to the outer world. I have referred to this as the vision–plan continuum: crafting a personal vision and creating a plan of action that will bring that vision into reality. Since our work as artists is firmly grounded in the ever-changing market place, we live our lives as entrepreneurs, responding in skillful and flexible ways, always mindful of synchronistic and serendipitous moments that serve to underscore our intentions. Because we understand the neuroplasticity of the brain and its regenerative capacities, we are able to reinvent ourselves as artists as we respond to changes in both our inner and outer circumstances.

Whether you are a performing artist, educator, director of a nonprofit, concert presenter, writer, scholar, or one who dreams of working in the music industry, this book has hopefully provided encouragement as well as strategies for creating your vision–plan continuum, your own musician's road map. Regardless of where you are in your professional life, you can move forward. The vast array of sources I have included in this book range from the wisdom of the ancient Greeks to modern business guides fresh off the press. Some of these sources, however, will become dated over time. In the music profession, the landscape can change quickly. Funding has its ebb and flow, new tools and technologies become available, and in rapid time our world can be quite different.

No one book, online source, or consultant can give you all the tools and information you need to launch your unique vision and plan. It's up to you to do the research and legwork. Remember, no one cares like you do about your own career! Central to your efforts will be building your network of contacts, broadening your skill base, developing a *flexible* business model, being mindful of the ever-changing market place, creating dynamic partnerships with individuals and institutions through effective consortia, and inviting to your work your own professional staff of advisers.

Although the music industry is in constant flux, the message of this book remains timeless for professionals, regardless of contemporary trends, economic conditions, or markets. The vision–plan can provide a way to discover your deepest artistic desires along with strategies to realize those dreams. This process is one that you will revisit throughout your lifetime. We launch our dreams, harvest the fruits of our work, and move on to new goals and visions. The vision–plan continuum can be a useful tool in living out this cyclical process, bringing you to an ever-expanding artistic life.

As you create your new musician's road map, you can connect with other artists and communities in building new arts consortia, offering urban and rural communities alike the gift of music. Through your work, you can bring into present time both the voices of living composers and those who have gone before, becoming a gateway to the numinous experience.

Musicians work in countless businesses, often creating their own independent enterprises as well as nonprofits. Whether you are an orchestra player, chair of the NEA, or working with underserved rural communities, the common thread is music. As musicians, we are here to share our talents and wisdom first with our local communities and then beyond. Without us, the music essentially remains on the page. Our work is truly a sacred service.

I offer this book as a catalyst for those in the music profession who aspire to expand their careers; to develop their artistry in new and authentic ways; to discover innovation in bringing music to live performance and historic recordings; to offer educational residencies that transform our public schools; and to realize in this process their own way of prevailing in this exquisite profession. *The Musician's Journey* can be the starting point as you begin your own transformation process.

Much of this book has addressed the concerns of the individual. One topic, however, remains to be explored. As individual musicians we are also part of a vast network of fellow professionals that serve the arts. From this group, we can draw resources, wisdom, collaboration, and regeneration. I call this collective world the musician's co-op.

In the 1970s, just on the tail end of the Hippie movement, co-ops were everywhere. There were co-op grocery stores, co-op newspapers, co-op childcare centers, and co-op housing. Essentially, a co-op is any kind of jointly owned commercial enterprise in which the participants, who are also owners, produce and distribute goods or services for mutual benefit. In other words, people band together to make their business operations more successful because together they have far greater resources compared to what only one person can provide. The whole is greater than the sum of its parts! This has direct bearing on how we thrive as musicians. Through cooperation with other artists we have first-hand access to ideas, resources, the all-important consortium, partnerships that share rather than duplicate assets, and a vast source of wisdom and enrichment. When we go it alone, we forever have to provide ourselves with everything required to manage our careers. By going solo in our efforts, we may very well miss crucial opportunities for valuable networking, professional engagements, and expanding our skill set. Understanding this concept of cooperation and collaboration is essential to the life of a thriving entrepreneur.

EPILOGUE

Once you are on your way, thriving in the musician's co-op, you are now in a position to empower others. Having had an awakening about new ways to prosper as a musician, you are in the proverbial catbird seat. Part of this positioning will inevitably be reflected in the teaching you do. Whether you are lecturing, giving master classes, working within the nonprofit sector, or pursing your own performing career, you can raise awareness by empowering others with the message of hope and inspiration. In a sense, we are all teachers. Vanda Scaravelli, in *Awakening the Spine*, eloquently describes the ideal:

> There are no good pupils, there are only good teachers. Teaching is not an imposition of the teacher's will over that of the pupil, not at all. Teaching starts with freedom and ends with freedom. A receptive state is required on the part of the pupil, a feeling of acceptance, even before the brain sees the truth of what is shown, an empty free space that one might call "innocence." It is from here that intelligence starts to function. The aim of the teacher is to awaken interest and curiosity in the mind of the pupil, giving him [her] a clear picture of the subject. His [her] explanations should be so evident and logical that the pupil cannot but grasp the significance of what is said. Understanding leads to independence and to freedom.[1]

From that place of freedom, we are able to bring the powerful message of music, and the arts for that matter, to others. From our co-op and the consortia we build, we can thrive in the music industry. We no longer rely on institutions for a single job, artistic identity, financial stability, or security. We know that our careers are firmly in our hands, that we have the resources and wisdom to prosper, and that our response to the global market place is grounded in flexibility, critical thinking, and adaptability. Our work becomes sustainable. And we may build the path as we go, while keeping a sharp eye out for synchronicity. As Dychtwald identifies, ultimately the unfolding of our careers will move us from success to significance: "Finding purpose in one's adult years is about many things—finding the job or pursuit of your dreams, replanting your time and money—and also developing the richest and most meaningful connections of your life, and through that support network reaching for your full potential."[2]

Whether you are in the midst of building your career, just starting out, or firmly established in your own professional pursuits, there is a common theme that can inspire you in how you view your work. My preferred focal point is on "gratitude." Out of gratitude and abundance we are poised, patient, and generous. In connecting with our world out of gratitude we join with others in the "co-op." We come to understand that there is plenty to go around.

Thriving entrepreneurs revel in sharing their talents and knowledge with others. From your own prosperous career, offer to others the gift of music. Plan your own philanthropy. It doesn't take much. Give a free concert every year or sponsor one that benefits the hungry, the homeless, or the disenfranchised. Consider raising money for disaster relief, or arts education in the schools. Help another artist on their path. Encourage a student. Provide hope and inspiration for other musicians who may have lost their way or have become discouraged. "For in every act of love and will—and in the long run they are both present in each genuine act—we mold ourselves and our world simultaneously. This is what it means to embrace the future."[3]

Those of us in the arts are sorely needed to make the world a better, more habitable place. Through the transcendent experience of music, we carry the torch of beauty, of universal truth, and human dignity. It is time to craft your vision and create your plan of action. Use passion to inspire you, humor to sustain you, and commitment to carry you forward. This is the musician's journey.

Notes

PREFACE

1. John Welwood, *Journey of the Heart: Intimate Relationship and the Path of Love* (San Francisco: HarperCollins, 1990), 34, 35.

CHAPTER 1

1. Rollo May, *The Courage to Create* (Gloucester, MA: Peter Smith, 1995), 45.

2. Chögyam Trungpa, *Shambhala: The Sacred Path of the Warrior* (Boston: Shambhala, 1988), 28.

3. Jaques Chailley, *40,000 Years of Music: Man in Search of Music* (New York: Da Capo, 1975), viii.

4. Peter Kalkavage, "The Neglected Music, Why Music Is an Essential Liberal Art," *American Educator* 30 (Fall 2006), 10.

5. Bill Ivey, "America Needs a New System for Supporting the Arts," *Chronicle of Higher Education* 51 (February 4, 2005), B9.

6. Robert A. Johnson, *Ecstasy: Understanding the Psychology of Joy* (New York: Harper and Row, 1987), 96.

7. Ibid., 87.

CHAPTER 2

1. James Mark Jordan, *The Musician's Soul: A Journey Examining Spirituality for Performers, Teachers, Composers, Conductors, and Music Educators* (Chicago: GIA Publications, 1999), 106.

2. John M. Eger, "Future Leaders Need Art-Infused Education," *San Diego Business Journal*, March 8, 2010, http://www.sdbj.com/news.

3. Bruce Duffie, "Interview with Gilbert Kalish," last modified 2009, http://www.bruceduffie. com/kalish.html.

CHAPTER 3

1. Hermann Hesse, "Stages" from *The Glass Bead Game: Magister Ludi* (New York: Henry Holt, 1990), 444. Copyright © 1990 by Herman Hesse. Reprinted by permission of Henry Holt and Company, LLC.

2. Small Business Association, Office of Advocacy, *Small Business Advocate* 18, no. 7 (August–September 2009): 5; http://www.sba.gov/sites/default/files/The%20Small%20Business%20 Advocate%20-%20August_September%202009.pdf

3. Gary D. Beckman, "Call for Papers—2007 Brevard Conference on Music Entrepreneurship," http://www.bcome.org/papers.html. Paraphrased from Beckman, Gary D. "'Adventuring' Arts Entrepreneurship Curricula in Higher Education: An Examination of Present Efforts, Obstacles and Best Practices." *Journal of Arts Management, Law & Society* 37, no. 2 (2007): 88–111.

4. Nancy Uscher, *Your Own Way in Music: A Career and Resource Guide* (New York: St. Martin's, 1990), 210.

CHAPTER 4

1. Thomas Münte, Eckart Altenmüller, and Lutz Jäncke, "The Musician's Brain as a Model of Neuroplasticity," *Nature Reviews Neuroscience* 2 (June 2002): 476.

2. Richard Davidson, "Neuroplasticity: Transforming the Mind by Changing the Brain," The Mind and Life Institute, October 18–22, 2004, http://www.mindandlife.org/pdfs/ml_12_brochure.pdf.

3. Glynda-Lee Hoffmann, *The Secret Dowry of Eve: Woman's Role in the Development of Consciousness* (Rochester, VT: Park Street, 2003), 54.

4. Ibid., 101.

5. Ibid., 103.

6. Ibid., 103–4.

7. Ibid., 96.

8. Oliver Sacks, *Musicophilia: Tales of Music and the Brain* (New York: Alfred A. Knopf, 2007), 300–301.

9. Hoffmann, *Secret Dowry*, 52.

10. Jordan, *Musician's Soul*, 50, 51.

11. Abraham Joshua Heschel, *God in Search of Man: A Philosophy of Judaism* (New York: Farrar, Straus and Giroux, 1983), 114–15.

12. Gary Zukav, *The Seat of the Soul* (New York: Simon and Schuster: Fireside, 1990), 189.

13. Ibid., 248.

14. Hoffmann, *Secret Dowry*, 195.

CHAPTER 5

1. Ira Progoff, trans. *The Cloud of Unknowing* (New York: Dell, 1989), 234.

2. Marion Woodman, *The Pregnant Virgin: A Process of Psychological Transformation* (Toronto, Canada: Inner City, 1985), 11.

3. Julia Cameron, *The Artist's Way: A Spiritual Path to Higher Creativity* (Los Angeles: Jeremy P. Tarcher/Perigee, 1992), xiii.

4. Abraham H. Maslow, *The Farther Reaches of Human Nature* (New York: Penguin, 1976), 90.

5. Oliver Sacks, "Tune in Your Head," *AARP Magazine* 51 (January–February 2008), 25.

6. Thomas Moore, *Care of the Soul: A Guide for Cultivating Depth and Sacredness in Everyday Life* (New York: HarperPerennial, 1994), xv.

7. Stanley Keleman, *Somatic Reality: Bodily Experience and Emotional Truth* (Berkeley: Center Press, 1979), 10.

8. Ibid., 12.

9. Ibid. 39.

10. Babette Rothschild, "Post-traumatic Stress Disorder: Identification and Diagnosis," *Soziale Arbeit Schweiz* [Swiss Journal of Social Work] (February 1998), 6.

11. Keleman, *Somatic Reality*, 105.

12. David Richo, *The Power of Coincidence: How Life Shows Us What We Need to Know* (Boston: Shambhala, 2007), 96.

13. Johnson, *Ecstasy*, 12.

CHAPTER 6

1. Howard Gardner, *Frames of Mind: The Theory of Multiple Intelligences,* 2nd ed. (New York: Basic Books, 2004), 69.

2. Angeles Arrien, "The Four-Fold Way," last modified December 1, 2011, http://www.ange-lesarrien.com/four-fol.htm.

3. Richo, *Power of Coincidence*, 92.

4. Diane Engle, *Sundials* (Concord, CA: Small Poetry Press, 2001), 31.

5. Elkhonon Goldberg, *The Wisdom Paradox: How Your Mind Can Grow Stronger as Your Brain Grows Older* (New York: Gotham, 2005), 352.

6. Dan Berrett, "The Myth of the Starving Artist," *Inside Higher Ed*, May 3, 2011, http://www.insidehighered.com/news/2011/05/03.

7. National Endowment for the Arts, "Artist Employment Projections Through 2018," Research Note 103, June 27, 2011, http://www.nea.gov/research/Notes/103.pdf.

CHAPTER 8

1. College Music Society, "Facts and Figures Concerning Music and Higher Education in the United States," last modified January 2012, http://www.music.org/cgi-bin/showpage.pl?tmpl=/outreach/highered/SumFacts&h=66.

CHAPTER 10

1. Vanda Scaravelli, *Awakening the Spine: The Stress-Free New Yoga that Works with the Body to Restore Health, Vitality, and Energy* (San Francisco: HarperSanFrancisco, 1991), 46.

2. Ken Dychtwald and Daniel J. Kadlec, *With Purpose: Going from Success to Significance in Work and Life* (New York: HarperCollins, 2009), 102.

3. Rollo May, *Love and Will* (New York: Norton, 1969), 325.

Selected Bibliography

Armstrong, Karen. *The Spiral Staircase: My Climb Out of Darkness*. New York: Alfred A. Knopf, 2004.

Arrien, Angeles. "The Four-Fold Way," last modified December 1, 2011, http://www.angelesarrien.com/four-fol.htm.

Auden, W. H. *The Complete Works of W. H. Auden*. Edited by Edward Mendelson. Princeton, NJ: Princeton University Press, 1996.

Autry, James A., and Stephen Mitchell. *Real Power: Business Lessons from the Tao Te Ching*. New York: Penguin Putnam, 1998.

Avanzini, Giuliano, Carmine Faienza, Diego Minciacchi, Luisa Lopez, and Maria Majno, eds. *The Neurosciences and Music*. Annals of the New York Academy of Sciences 999. New York: New York Academy of Sciences, 2003.

Barrell, M. Kay. *The Technical Production Handbook*. Salt Lake City: Publisher's Press, 1991.

Beckman, Gary D. "'Adventuring' Arts Entrepreneurship Curricula in Higher Education: An Examination of Present Efforts, Obstacles, and Best Practices." *Journal of Arts Management, Law & Society* 37, no. 2 (2007).

Beckman, Gary D., ed. *Disciplining the Arts: Teaching Entrepreneurship in Context*. New York: Rowman and Littlefield Education, 2011.

Beeching, Angela. *Beyond Talent: Creating a Successful Career in Music*. 2nd ed. New York: Oxford University Press, 2010.

Benton, Thomas H. "Leaving the Village." *Chronicle of Higher Education,* February 13, 2006, C1.

Bernstein, Seymour. *With Your Own Two Hands: Self-Discovery through Music*. New York: Schirmer, 1981.

Berrett, Dan. "The Myth of the Starving Artist," *Inside Higher Ed*, May 3, 2011, http://www.insidehighered.com/news/2011/05/03.

Bly, Robert, and Marion Woodman. *The Maiden King: The Reunion of Masculine and Feminine.* New York: Henry Holt, 1998.

Bolen, Jean Shinoda. *The Tao of Psychology: Synchronicity and the Self.* San Francisco: Harper and Row, 1979.

——. *Close to the Bone: Life-Threatening Illness and the Search for Meaning.* New York: Simon and Schuster, 1998.

Bolles, Richard N. *What Color Is Your Parachute? A Manual for Job-Hunters and Career-Changers.* "Hard Times" Edition. Berkeley: Ten Speed, 2012.

Branden, Nathaniel. *The Six Pillars of Self-Esteem.* New York: Bantam, 1994.

Branden, Nathaniel. *The Art of Living Consciously: The Power of Awareness to Transform Everyday Life.* New York: Simon and Schuster, 1999.

Brauer, David. "Get Your Resume Right." *My Generation* (September–October 2002): 28.

Brewster, David. "The Case for Festivals." *Seattle Weekly*, June 4–10, 1986, 41.

Bridges, William. *Transitions: Making Sense of Life's Changes.* New York: Addison-Wesley, 1980.

Brinckman, Jonathan. "Referral Program Keeps Sales Bubbling." *Oregonian* (Portland, OR), May 31, 2004.

Brown, Steven, and Lawrence M. Parsons. "The Neuroscience of Dance." *Scientific American* 299 (July 2008): 78.

Cameron, Julia. *The Artist's Way: A Spiritual Path to Higher Creativity.* Los Angeles: Jeremy P. Tarcher/Perigee, 1992.

Campbell, Joseph. *The World of Joseph Campbell.* Vol. 3, *The Western Way: Transformations of Myth through Time.* St. Paul: HighBridge, 1990.

Campbell, Joseph, Bill D. Moyers, and Betty S. Flowers. *The Power of Myth.* New York: Anchor, 1991.

Carhart, Thaddeus. *The Piano Shop on the Left Bank.* New York: Random House, 2001.

Carlson, Richard. *Don't Sweat the Small Stuff with Your Family: Simple Ways to Keep Daily Responsibilities and Household Chaos from Taking Over Your Life.* New York: Hyperion, 1998.

Carter, Steven. "Turning to Teaching." *Oregonian* (Portland, OR), November 7, 1999, 3M.

Chailley, Jacques. *40,000 Years of Music: Man in Search of Music.* New York: Da Capo, 1975.

Chandler, Stephanie. *From Entrepreneur to Infopreneur: Make Money with Books, E-books, and Other Information Products.* Hoboken: John Wiley and Sons, 2007.

——. *Own Your Niche: Hype-Free Internet Marketing Tactics to Establish Authority in Your Field and Promote Your Service-Based Business.* Gold River, CA: Authority Publishing. 2012.

Chödrön, Pema. *The Places that Scare You: A Guide to Fearlessness in Difficult Times.* Boston: Shambhala, 2002.

Chopra, Deepak. *The Seven Spiritual Laws of Success: A Practical Guide to the Fulfillment of Your Dreams.* San Rafael, CA: Amber-Allen, 1994.

Churnin, Nancy. "Scientists Rethinking the Brain." *Oregonian* (Portland, OR), March 17, 2010, C2.

College Music Society. "Facts and Figures Concerning Music and Higher Education in the United States," last modified January 2012, http://www.music.org/cgi-bin/showpage.pl?tmpl=/outreach/highered/SumFacts&h=66.

Collins, Billy. *Sailing Alone Around the Room: New and Selected Poems.* New York: Random House, 2002.

Covey, Stephen R. *Principle-Centered Leadership*. New York: Free Press, 2003.

———. *First Things First*. New York: Free Press, 2003.

Cummings, Charles. *Spirituality and the Desert Experience*. Denville, NJ: Dimension Books, 1978.

Dalai Lama [Tenzin Gyatso]. *Many Ways to Nirvana: Reflections on Right Living*. Edited by Renuka Singh. New York: Penguin Compass, 2005.

Davidson, Richard. "Neuroplasticity: Transforming the Mind by Changing the Brain," Mind and Life Institute, October 18–22, 2004; http://www.mindandlife.org/pdfs/ml_12_brochure.pdf.

Dominguez, Joe, and Vicki Robin. *Your Money or Your Life: Transforming Your Relationship with Money and Achieving Financial Independence*. 3rd ed. New York: Penguin Books, 1999.

Duffie, Bruce. "Interview with Gilbert Kalish," last modified 2009, http://www.bruceduffie.com/kalish.html.

Dychtwald, Ken, and Daniel J. Kadlec. *With Purpose: Going from Success to Significance in Work and Life*. New York: HarperCollins, 2009.

Dyer, Wayne W. *Change Your Thoughts, Change Your Life: Living the Wisdom of the Tao*. Carlsbad, CA: Hay House, 2007.

———. *The Power of Intention: Learning to Co-create Your World Your Way*. Rev. ed. Carlsbad, CA: Hay House, 2010.

Edwards, Sarah, and Paul Edwards. *Secrets of Self-Employment: Surviving and Thriving on the Ups and Downs of Being Your Own Boss*. New York: G. P. Putnam's Sons, 1996.

Eger, John M. "Future Leaders Need Art-Infused Education," *San Diego Business Journal*, March 8, 2010, http://www.sdbj.com/news.

Eisenson, Marc, Gerri Detweiller, and Nancy Castleman. *Invest In Yourself: Six Secrets to a Rich Life*. New York: John Wiley and Sons, 1998.

Ellison, Katherine. "Mastering Your Own Mind." *Psychology Today* (September–October 2006): 70; http://www.psychologytoday.com/articles/200608/mastering-your-own-mind.

Engle, Diane. *Sundials*. Concord, CA: Small Poetry Press, 2001.

Filips, Janet. "Heavy Mental." *Oregonian* (Portland, OR), December 12, 1988, D1.

Fish, Robert. *Job Hunting A to Z: Landing the Job You Want*. San Francisco: WetFeet, 2005.

Fromm, Erich. *To Have or To Be?* Rev. ed. London; New York: Continuum, 2010.

Fuller, R. Buckminster. *Operating Manual for Spaceship Earth*. New Ed. Baden, Switzerland: Lars Müller, 2008.

Gardner, Howard. *Frames of Mind: The Theory of Multiple Intelligences*. 2nd ed. New York: Basic Books, 2004.

Gawain, Shakti. *Creative Visualization: Use the Power of Your Imagination to Create What You Want in Your Life*. 30th anniversary ed. Novato, CA: Nataraj; Enfield, UK: Publishers Group, 2009.

Glass, Lillian. *Toxic People: 10 Ways of Dealing with People Who Make Your Life Miserable*. New York: St. Martin's/Griffin, 1997.

Goldberg, Elkhonon. *The Executive Brain: Frontal Lobes and the Civilized Mind*. New York: Oxford University Press, 2001.

———. *The Wisdom Paradox: How Your Mind Can Grow Stronger as Your Brain Grows Older*. New York: Gotham, 2005.

Goleman, Daniel. *Emotional Intelligence: Why It Can Matter More Than IQ.* New York: Bantam, 1997.

Goodman, Ellen, and Patricia O'Brien. *I Know Just What You Mean: The Power of Friendship in Women's Lives.* New York: Simon and Schuster, 2000.

Graves, Bill. "Top Educator Picks Apart the System." *Oregonian* (Portland, OR), November 7, 2000, E4.

Grudin, Robert. *Time and the Art of Living.* 2nd ed. New York: Ticknor and Fields, 1988.

Gumpert, David E. *How to Really Create a Successful Business Plan: Step-by-Step Guide.* Needham, MA: Lauson Publishing Co., 2003.

Halpern, Jake. "The Passions and Privations of the Start-Up Entrepreneur." *Yale Alumni Magazine* 73 (January–February 2010): 33.

Hanh, Thich Nhat, and Rachel Neumann. *Being Peace.* Rev. ed. Berkeley: Parallax, 2005.

Hart, Mickey. *Drumming at the Edge of Magic: A Journey into the Spirit of Percussion.* San Francisco: HarperCollins, 1990.

Herrigel, Eugen and R. F. C. Hull. *Zen in the Art of Archery.* London: Penguin Books, 2004.

Heschel, Abraham Joshua. *God in Search of Man: A Philosophy of Judaism.* New York: Farrar, Straus and Giroux, 1983.

Hesse, Hermann. *The Glass Bead Game: Magister Ludi.* New York: Henry Holt, 1990.

Hicks, Bob. "Art for All, and All for Art." *Oregonian* (Portland, OR), February 2, 2003, D1.

Hoffmann, Glynda-Lee. *The Secret Dowry of Eve: Woman's Role in the Development of Consciousness.* Rochester, VT: Park Street, 2003.

Holland, Eloise. "Climbing to the Top." *Portland Community College Communities* [Portland, OR] 23 (Spring 2010): 6.

Hollis, James. *The Middle Passage: From Misery to Meaning in Midlife.* Toronto: Inner City, 1993.

———. *Under Saturn's Shadow: The Wounding and Healing of Men.* Toronto: Inner City, 1994.

———. *The Eden Project: In Search of the Magical Other.* Toronto: Inner City, 1997.

———. *Finding Meaning in the Second Half of Life: How to Finally, Really Grow Up.* New York: Penguin, 2005

Huff, Priscilla Y. *HerVenture.com: Your Guide to Expanding Your Small or Home Business to the Internet, Easily and Profitably.* Roseville, CA: Prima Soho, 2000.

Hurley, Kathleen, and Theodore Dobson. *My Best Self: Using the Enneagram to Free the Soul.* San Francisco: HarperCollins, 1993.

Huxley, Aldous. *Island.* New York: Harper and Row, 1962.

Hyde, Lewis. *The Gift: Creativity and the Artist in the Modern World.* New York: Harper and Row, 2007.

Ivey, Bill. "America Needs a New System for Supporting the Arts." *Chronicle of Higher Education* 51 (February 4, 2005): B6.

Johnson, Robert A. *Ecstasy: Understanding the Psychology of Joy.* New York: Harper and Row, 1987.

Johnson, Robert A. *Lying with the Heavenly Woman: Understanding and Integrating the Feminine Archetypes in Men's Lives.* San Francisco: HarperCollins, 1994.

Johnson, Robert A., and Jerry M. Ruhl. *Contentment: A Way to True Happiness.* New York: HarperCollins, 1999.

Jordan, James Mark. *The Musician's Soul: A Journey Examining Spirituality for Performers, Teachers, Composers, Conductors, and Music Educators.* Chicago: GIA Publications, 1999.

Kalkavage, Peter. "The Neglected Music, Why Music Is an Essential Liberal Art." *American Educator* 30 (Fall 2006): 10.

Keleman, Stanley. *Somatic Reality: Bodily Experience and Emotional Truth.* Berkeley: Center Press, 1979.

Kornfield, Jack. *A Path with Heart: A Guide through the Perils and Promises of Spiritual Life.* New York: Bantam, 1993.

Levoy, Gregg. *Callings: Finding and Following an Authentic Life.* New York: Three Rivers, 1997.

Martin, Sara. "Music Lessons Enhance Spatial Reasoning Skills." *American Psychological Association Monitor* 25 (October 1994): 5.

Maslow, Abraham H. *The Farther Reaches of Human Nature.* New York: Penguin, 1976.

———. *Religions, Values, and Peak-Experiences.* New York: Penguin, 1976.

———. *Toward a Psychology of Being.* Eastford, CT: Martino Publishing, 2010.

Mayer, Nancy. "A Mentor's Hand Can Guide Career." *Oregonian* (Portland, OR), May 28, 2000, L13.

May, Rollo. *Love and Will.* New York: Norton, 1969.

———. *The Courage to Create.* Gloucester, MA: Peter Smith, 1995.

———. *Freedom and Destiny.* New York: Norton, 1999.

McDaniel, Nello, and George Thorn. *Learning Audiences: Adult Arts Participation and the Learning Consciousness: The Final Report of the Adult Arts Education Project.* Washington, DC: John F. Kennedy Center for the Performing Arts, 1997.

Miller, Lee E. *Get More Money on Your Next Job...in Any Economy.* New York: McGraw-Hill, 2009.

Mitchell, Stephen. *Tao Te Ching: A New English Version.* New York: Harper and Row, 1988.

Mitchner, Ted. "Attitude Helps in Quest for New Job." *Oregonian* (Portland, OR), September 22, 2002, G1.

———. "Enthusiasm Boosts Employability." *Oregonian* (Portland, OR), September 8, 2002, G1.

———. "Shift Makes Time for Her First Love." *Oregonian* (Portland, OR), September 12, 2004, G1.

Montparker, Carol. "Following the Path of Opportunity." *Clavier* 32 (May–June 1993): 10–14.

Moore, Robert, and Douglas Gillette. *King, Warrior, Magician, Lover: Rediscovering the Archetypes of the Mature Masculine.* New York: HarperCollins, 1990.

Moore, Thomas. *Care of the Soul: A Guide for Cultivating Depth and Sacredness in Everyday Life.* New York: HarperPerennial, 1994.

———. *Original Self: Living with Paradox and Originality.* New York: HarperCollins, 2000.

———. *A Life at Work: The Joy of Discovering What You Were Born to Do.* New York: Broadway, 2008.

Moss, Richard. *The Black Butterfly: An Invitation to Radical Aliveness.* Berkeley: Celestial Arts, 1986.

Münte, Thomas, Eckart Altenmüller, and Lutz Jäncke. "The Musician's Brain as a Model of Neuroplasticity." *Nature Reviews Neuroscience* 3 (June 2002): 473–78.

Myss, Caroline M. *Anatomy of the Spirit.* New York: Three Rivers, 1996.

———. *Invisible Acts of Power: Channeling Grace in Your Everyday Life*. New York: Free Press, 2006.

National Endowment for the Arts, "Artist Employment Projections Through 2018," Research Note 103, June 27, 2011, http://www.nea.gov/research/Notes/103.pdf.

Otto, Rudolf. *The Idea of the Holy*. New York: Oxford University Press, 1958.

Parlapiano, Ellen H., and Patricia Cobe. *Mompreneurs: A Mother's Practical Step-by-Step Guide to Work-at-Home Success*. New York: Perigee, 1996.

Peck, M. Scott. *Further Along the Road Less Traveled*. New York: Simon and Schuster, 1993.

Pink, Daniel. *A Whole New Mind: Why Right-Brainers Will Rule the Future*. New York: Penguin, 2006.

Progoff, Ira, trans. *The Cloud of Unknowing*. New York: Dell, 1989.

Rice-See, Lynn. "A Delicate Balance: A Study of Professional Lives of Piano Faculty in Higher Education." *American Music Teacher* 53, no.1 (2003): 30–36.

Richo, David. *The Five Things We Cannot Change…and the Happiness We Find by Embracing Them*. Boston: Shambhala, 2006.

———. *The Power of Coincidence: How Life Shows Us What We Need to Know*. Boston: Shambhala, 2007.

Riggott, Julie. "With a Song in Their Hearts." *USC Trojan Family Magazine* 41 (Winter 2009): 28.

Riso, Don Richard. *Discovering Your Personality Type: The New Enneagram Questionnaire*. Boston: Houghton Mifflin, 1995.

Ristad, Eloise. *A Soprano on Her Head*. Moab, UT: Real People, 1982.

Robbins, John. *The New Good Life: Living Better Than Ever in an Age of Less*. New York: Ballantine, 2010.

Rohr, Richard. *The Naked Now: Learning to See as the Mystics See*. New York: Crossroads, 2009.

Rothschild, Babette. "Post-traumatic Stress Disorder: Identification and Diagnosis." *Soziale Arbeit Schweiz* [Swiss Journal of Social Work] (February 1998): 6.

Ruiz, Don Miguel. *The Four Agreements: A Practical Guide to Personal Freedom*. San Rafael, CA: Amber-Allen, 1997.

Russell, Bertrand. *The Conquest of Happiness*. Introduction by Anthony C. Grayling. London: Routledge, 2010.

Sacks, Oliver. *Musicophilia: Tales of Music and the Brain*. New York: Alfred A. Knopf, 2007.

———. "Tune in Our Head." *AARP Magazine* 51(January–February 2008): 25.

Sagan, Carl. *Pale Blue Dot: A Vision of the Human Future in Space*. New York: Ballantine, 1994.

Scaravelli, Vanda. *Awakening the Spine: The Stress-Free New Yoga that Works with the Body to Restore Health, Vitality, and Energy*. San Francisco: HarperSanFrancisco, 1991.

Schaef, Anne Wilson. *When Society Becomes an Addict*. New York: Harper and Row, 1987.

Schmid, Randolph E. "Research Finds Brain Link for Words, Music." *Seattle Times*, February 21, 2010, A8.

Sher, Barbara, and Barbara Smith. *I Could Do Anything If I Only Knew What It Was: How to Discover What You Really Want and How to Get It*. New York: Delacorte, 1994.

Sine, Christine. *Sacred Rhythms: Finding a Peaceful Pace in a Hectic World*. Grand Rapids: Baker, 2003.

Sinetar, Marsha. *Do What You Love, the Money Will Follow: Discovering Your Right Livelihood.* New York: Dell, 1989.

Small, Jacquelyn. *Awakening in Time: The Journey from Codependence to Co-creation.* New York: Bantam, 1991.

Small Business Association, Office of Advocacy. *Small Business Advocate* 18, no. 7 (August–September 2009): 5; http://www.sba.gov/sites/default/files/The%20Small%20Business%20Advocate%20-%20August_September%202009.pdf

Steinbrenner, Corinne. "Big Dreams, Small Budgets." *Esprit* (Boston University College of Fine Arts) (Winter 2010): 14.

St. James, Elaine. *Simplify Your Life: 100 Ways to Slow Down and Enjoy the Things that Really Matter.* New York: Hyperion, 1994.

Suzuki, Daisetz Teitaro and Christmas Humphreys. *The Awakening of Zen.* Boston: Shambhala, 2000.

Tallmadge, Alice. "Rich Strive to Keep Values Intact as They Give to Causes." *Oregonian* (Portland, OR), May 21, 2000, E8.

Taylor, Bruce D. *The Arts Equation: Forging a Vital Link between Performing Artists and Educators.* New York: Backstage Books, 1999.

Thoreau, Henry D. *Walden and Other Writings.* New York: Bantam 2004.

Tillich, Paul. *The New Being.* Lincoln: University of Nebraska Press, 2005.

Tolle, Eckhart. *The Power of Now: A Guide to Spiritual Enlightenment.* Sydney: Hachette, 2011.

Trungpa, Chögyam. *Shambhala: The Sacred Path of the Warrior.* Boston: Shambhala, 1988.

Uscher, Nancy. *Your Own Way in Music: A Career and Resource Guide.* New York: St. Martin's, 1990.

Walker, Alan. "Music and Education." *Piano Quarterly* 148 (1981): 25–27.

Watts, Alan W. *The Wisdom of Insecurity.* London: Rider, 1978.

———. *The Book: On the Taboo Against Knowing Who You Are.* London: Souvenir, 2009.

Welwood, John. *Journey of the Heart: Intimate Relationship and the Path of Love.* San Francisco: HarperCollins, 1990.

White, John. "Empty Hand, Empty Self." *Yoga Journal* 99 (July–August 1991): 20–22.

Winter, Barbara J. *Making a Living without a Job: Winning Ways for Creating Work that You Love.* New York: Bantam, 1993.

Woodman, Marion. *The Pregnant Virgin: A Process of Psychological Transformation.* Toronto, Canada: Inner City, 1985.

Woodman, Marion, and Jill Mellick. *Coming Home to Myself: Daily Reflections for a Woman's Body and Soul.* Berkeley: Conari, 1998.

Woodward, Steve. "Stop Kvetching and Show Some Chutzpah." *Oregonian* (Portland, OR), March 2, 2003, L1.

Wortham, Jenna. "More Employers Use Social Networks to Check Out Applicants." *New York Times*, August 20, 2009, http://bits.blogs.nytimes.com/2009/08/20/more-employers-use-social-networks-to-check-out-applicants/?em.

Zukav, Gary. *The Seat of the Soul.* New York: Simon and Schuster: Fireside, 1990.

Index